RADICAL MANAGEMENT

RADICAL MANAGEMENT
Power Politics
and
the Pursuit of Trust

Samuel A. Culbert
John J. McDonough

THE FREE PRESS
A Division of Macmillan, Inc.
NEW YORK

Collier Macmillan Publishers
LONDON

The Free Press
A Division of Macmillan, Inc.
866 Third Avenue, New York, N.Y. 10022

Collier Macmillan Canada, Inc.

Printed in the United States of America

printing number

1 2 3 4 5 6 7 8 9 10

Library of Congress Cataloging in Publication Data

Culbert, Samuel A.
    Radical management.

    I. Management.   I. McDonough, John J. (John Joseph).
II. Title.
HD31.C8 1985   658   85–10150
ISBN 978-1-4165-7643-3   ISBN 1-4165-7643-6

With love to
Anne, John, and Elaine
and to
Charles, Gar, Samantha, and Mary

Contents

Preface

Once again we claim to have written our "last" book. We think this one takes an essential step in communicating our message broadly—that there is an inherently political dimension to one's everyday participation at work and that this dimension requires constant monitoring and attention. We're hoping that our thesis becomes a reference that people will point to in specifying the type of sensitivity and consciousness they would like to see added in the workplace. Our logic flows like this:

1. Trusting relationships are a necessary condition for the long-term effectiveness of any organization.

2. The Human Relations people were right, communication skills and empathy are the keys to trusting relationships.

3. *But*, before good communications leading to trusting relationships are possible, one first has to recognize the political forces that are inherent in any situation, and then one must deal skillfully with them.

Our book is about the political dynamics inherent in every organizational situation and what needs to be understood before people can form trusting relationships. When the politics are not addressed, good intentions and good-enough communication skills don't work. The resulting structure simply makes it impossible for people to form trusting relationships. And we find that what most people understand about the political forces that accompany any organizational situation wouldn't fill the proverbial thimble.

This book is written for accomplished managers, prospective managers, and academics alike. We are management educators who, through our consulting and involvement in the business community, have developed perspectives that add a missing dimension to the practical, analytic, bottom-line–oriented thinking that managers use today. We are also researchers whose mode of inquiry has led to a theory and distinctive viewpoint that we would like to have known and appreciated by our peers. And we are university professors with concerns that our students acquire the perspectives needed to succeed in established organizations, and on terms that are personally meaningful to them.

In writing this book, as well as the two that preceded it, we gave a great deal of thought to identifying a mode of presentation that would appeal to our three target audiences simultaneously. At the same time, we wanted to observe the tenets of thoughtful clinical inquiry and to put our ideas in a form to which experienced managers could personally relate and that newcomers could visualize and understand. Of course we also sought a lively presentation mode that would hold people's interests, for we recognized that our perspective requires immersion in an interlocking set of concepts that are not easily broken down into a discrete and linear list of ideas.

For us, the common denominator is each individual's own personal experience. We present, as our format for analysis and documentation, case situations and work-life vignettes selected for their ability to illustrate our points in contexts to which people in different situations can personally relate. After all, when it counts, personal experience is what people rely on anyway. Personal experience is what accomplished managers rely on when under pressure, proceeding in waters they deem hazardous, and it is what academic researchers fall back on when encountering theories with conflicting, and substantiated, conclusions. What's more, we find that this is what the management neophyte trusts. While our students lack work experience, they all have life experiences that in their minds parallel what they anticipate facing when they begin their professional work.

Of course everyone knows that there is no way of presenting a case or of describing an organization event that is totally objective or will accurately reflect the observations and experience of each person who witnessed it. This is the well-documented *Rashomon**effect. Each participant sees events differently and ascribes different meanings to what he or she observes. So while we do our best to present accounts that portray situations as we actually witnessed them, we do not base the validity of our conclusions on any assumption that another team of viewers would see the same events exactly as we describe them, or interpret their meaning as we did, or even that they would choose the same event to make the point we selected it to illustrate.

The validation for what we assert rests in the mind of each reader. Does what we assert and our illustration of it fit with your experience? Do you find our conclusions plausible? Do you see parallels in your own life and in your own work experiences to what we have seen and assert? And, most important, do our perspectives help you to see facets of familiar events that you have previously missed and do you believe what we have concluded will help you deal more effectively with the organization events you face tomorrow?

We contend that what we have to say—the perspectives we draw from the situations we relate and the theories we illustrate with them—should stand the test of each reader's personal experience. If it does, our viewpoint has passed one of the most crucial tests of scientific credibility. We invite readers to reflect on the events we describe and to relate them to their own experiences, whatever those experiences may have been, with all the idiosyncratic and special biases in interpretation that one gives to them, and to conduct their own tests of validity. What we assert should either prove personally valid or it should be discarded.

However, keep in mind that people can sometimes be deceived by their experience. Every culture and organization socializes its members to receive their experience in mainstream categories that

---

*Rashomon is a classic Japanese film that graphically depicts how differences in lifestyle and motivation cause participants to experience the same event differently.

do not accurately represent one's personal reaction. For instance, in the 1970s there were groups of people, even entire companies, who thought that a managerial technique called "management-by-objectives" could enforce responsible participation. This technique became "valid" to the extent that an estimated 40 percent of the *Fortune* 500 companies instituted management effectiveness programs based on it. And in the 1980s the majority of these programs have fallen by the wayside, leaving many who participated more aware of its flaws than its strengths. Yes, it is possible to convince an entire group of a "fact" that later becomes invalid. So while we encourage people to use their own experience as a base, we also caution them not to rubber stamp their subjective reactions.

But would other, more objective modes of inquiry better protect people from accepting an invalid "fact" than would a subjective reading of one's own personal experience? We don't know— it's possible. Certainly traditional modes of research and scientific inquiry are invaluable. On the other hand, when it comes to social and psychological facts, the method of inquiry and the mode of verification must be matched with the question raised. When the question deals with the nature of an organization's reality, then the search must include the subjective needs of the individuals who assert conflicting realities. Unlike the physical sciences, in management one seldom finds an invariant order that is independent of the individuals who experience it. Thus we believe that the principles put forth in this book are best validated in the experience of the reader and adapted to the specific situation faced.

Acknowledgments

In our consulting we're often in the position of advising managers-who-know-better to pay attention to something basic which, for one reason or another, they overlooked. Over the years we've learned to deliver our comments with tact. We've learned that being too direct can prove dysfunctional, preoccupying managers with the need to justify their omissions instead of just relating to the usefulness of what we seek to add.

Writing this book put us on the other side of the desk. In effect, we were in the role of a manager missing something he knew better than to overlook. Now's our chance to thank our tactful friends and associates, whose critique and commentary helped reacquaint us with what we, along the way, inadvertently overlooked.

Torie Osborn was our editor. She quickly caught on that we can't tolerate fine-tuning until our "big picture" is engaged. Torie is a sensitive woman with an extraordinary capacity for reading concepts through verbal camouflage. Not only did her work add clarity to the line-by-line flow of words and ideas you are about to read, but her spirited presence brought respite from the loneliness of a writing day.

Harold Roth was and is our agent. He's a kind, intelligent man who tactfully, but strongly, pursues an idea until one relates squarely to his point. Harold was wonderfully generous with his involvement, and we sincerely hope that the friendship and respect that resulted lasts long after his last royalty check is cashed.

There are friends who now have become "regulars" whom we thank with every book. Max Elden, Oscar Ortsman, Warren Bennis, Allen Koplin, and Mort Lachman read preliminary chapter drafts. Each of these men is a distinguished professional with a developed viewpoint and unique perspective. We feel fortunate to have had their feedback, for our process and thinking benefited greatly from their reactions.

There was a time when we were so convinced we had the correct chapter organization, if not the optimum wording, that we called a meeting of some of our most trusted friends and asked them to "sock it to us" directly. Each dutifully read our manuscript and came prepared for an all-day meeting. We began by begging them to be direct and assuring them that we needed as much candor as possible. We apparently did such a good job of *convincing them* that the conversation went two hours before someone felt sufficiently brave to venture a criticism. The ensuing discussion proved enlightening and resulted in an entire redraft. For their participation and considerate candor we thank Howard Carr, Herb Kindler, Ilene Kahn, David Boje, Carol Carothers, Paul Heckman, Dick Elpers, Mark Pisano, Yvonne Randle, and Terry Wolfe.

There were other friends and work associates whose reading and philosophical discussions helped more than they would ever suspect. Lengthy discussions and project work with Monte Strauss, Bill Broesamle, and Howard Carr were tremendously important. Discussions with Borah Perlmutter, Karen Thomas, Terence Krell, Rex Mitchell, and Loyd Forrest helped enormously. Artistic ideas were contributed by Jay Beynon and Jackie Barry; professional encouragement by Walter Nord, Peter Frost, Robert Poupart, Dennis Holmes, Steve McKee, Peter Hoffman, Stan Holditch, and Richard Kirshberg; and secretarial and wor processing (sic) assistance from Irv Powell, Ruth Zartler, Mary Sanchez, and the word processing group at our Graduate School of Management.

We feel it is important to acknowledge our intellectual debt and gratitude to three very important figures in the field of organization behavior—Warren Bennis, Chris Argyris, and Bob Tannenbaum. More than any in our field, Warren and Chris have been willing to tackle head-on the tough issues concerning the integration of the individual and the organization and to detail the human costs of operating with an overly rationalistic model of how an organization should run. For years Bob Tannenbaum has served, for us, as a model of intellectual honesty and moral courage, as someone to emulate in bringing our professional behavior up to the level of our value commitments and theory.

Finally, we are delighted to have the chance to thank our wives Elaine McDonough and Mary Beaudry-Culbert in print. Each contributed love and support and gave their feedback on our writing as tactfully as they could, considering that for four years this book was "the other woman." Mary even took on some of the formal editing and invested days looking for the flaws in logic and clarity which we and our editor Torie had overlooked. Mary was seldom critical of us. Instead, she would dismiss our oversights by saying, "What else can you expect from three Leos with the same birthday!" Of course, from her comment, anyone would know that Mary is a Taurus born on the Gemini cusp.

Introduction

CHAPTER 1

The Subjective Element

Something is radically wrong with the mind-set that is being used at work. People are using an overly rational approach that implies more logic and objectivity than what actually exists. What is taking place is far more personal, far more subjective, and far more power-oriented and political than most popular theories lead one to expect. Managers control others far less than their words, plans, and actions imply. Systems and procedures are determined far more by personality and hard-fought compromise than the logical explanations used to describe and justify them would ever lead one to believe.

This book is aimed at updating contemporary management beliefs and practices. Its goal is to provide the insights and perspectives that allow managers to recast organizational events in ways that account for the subjective element—that which actually determines how people see events, do their jobs, and transact with others. Everyone knows about the presence of subjective forces, but we find that what most people know doesn't make much of a difference. We have a perspective that will make it much easier for today's management to comprehend what is subjective and political in the workplace—and to deal with it above-board and directly.

We decided to name this book *Radical Management* to underscore the extent of the change that is needed. And we use the term "radical" not as a dismissal of the past or to connote far-out modes of operating, but as a signal that now is the time to reassess the roles people and their subjective involvements play in creating organizational systems, and to encourage managers to seek alternatives to current self-limiting practices. *Radical Management* is our term for urging people to think more basically, to depart from present practices, and to consider alternative frameworks that take more account of the subjective forces that are part and parcel of each work event. People need to develop their capacities for reasoning from needs they see the system experiencing and from needs they see individuals experiencing to come up with new and more complete statements of problems. They also need to develop their capacities to reason from agreed-upon statements of problems to come up with new approaches and solutions that take more account of what is subjective.

Basic to this book's perspective are ideas for coping with *organizational politics*, which we think is a given in any organization and which people must learn how to deal with positively; ideas for promoting *trusting relationships*, which we claim is the most efficient management tool ever invented; and ideas for pursuing the *contexts* which make one's actions understandable, useful, and organizationally valued. All of these ideas depend on understanding and inclusion of the subjective element.

But including the subjective element presents problems for a lot of people. It involves a way of reasoning that many find inefficient; it involves issues that many feel incompetent to handle; and, it involves a mode of thinking that runs counter to the overly objective conceptualizations that most people are accustomed to using. In fact we have discovered that the majority of people who downplay the importance of subjective considerations privately agree with statements of its importance but continue in the conventional mode for fear of assuming an orientation that will make them appear ineffective. Many would rather continue with misconceived orientations that allow them to appear competent than pursue a more valid course and risk not having the skills required to ensure its success.

The way we see it, the next wave of management thinking must include a perspective that will make it possible for managers to penetrate existing modes of reasoning to accomplish some things that current rationalistic approaches do not permit. It will have to be different because there is a class of high priority issues that resist solution even though they are the subject of constant managerial concern. Managers don't know how to switch tracks in dealing with them and we suspect that the conventional way of approaching these issues is a large part of why they resist solution. Major discrepancies are being raised but they are just not getting resolved. For instance:

- Despite all the rhetoric about human relations and the importance of communications, people experience power and hierarchy as far and away the most dominant forces in management today.

- Despite all efforts to pay people fairly and reward them for accomplishment and technical know-how, people increasingly believe that their rewards are dependent on organization politics where who you know and what they think of you are more important than actual contribution.

- Despite the fact that people want to belong to an organization in which they can believe and to which they can be loyal and sacrifice, on a daily basis they believe it is loyalty to the boss and not loyalty to the company that gets rewarded.

- Despite open-door policies and statements by higher-ups that they want candid reports of what people actually think, few people believe they can tell it straight with confidence that their organization will tolerate their criticisms without costs to them.

- Despite the fact that managers are encouraged to compete and fight hard for what they believe, too often those who compete wind up in disrespectful and destructive relationships and, worst of all, they don't seem to learn from considering the substance of what their adversaries put forth.

- Despite the efforts of many companies to stream-line their management structure and to promote a spirit of entrepreneurship within the ranks, there are too many instances of overly cautious behavior that managers justify on the basis of the shabby treatment unsuccessful risk-takers receive.

- Despite pleas to middle and lower level management to think strategically and to build a long-term perspective into their unit's operations, these same people claim they are prevented

from doing so by upper level executives whose year-end bo-
nuses depend on short-term results and whose peace of
mind depends on producing the quarterly increases in profit
that keep speculation-oriented stockholders off their backs.

We wouldn't worry about discrepancies like these if we
thought people were making progress. And their inability to solve
them is not for lack of resources expended. In fact the back-up
strategy for dealing with each of these discrepancies unfortunately appears to be longer and stronger with the same inadequate approach. No, more energy and more of the same type of
resources are not going to fix discrepancies like these. But, we believe, different managerial reasoning will.

Our own view of management, and of the central role subjectivity plays in determining the course of organization events, has
evolved over many years of consulting and being called upon to
help managers deal with controversy and conflict in their efforts
to develop more effective teamwork. Of course, such situations
provide natural opportunities for us, as university professors and
researchers, to analyze the structures that produce the problems
we are hired to fix. They also provide opportunities to put theories we espouse in the classroom to their practical test. Thus our
efforts to build teamwork and our theorizing about what managers need to learn to create more teamwork on their own have
gone through a process of evolution until we arrived at where we
are today.

Initially we took a human relations approach. Communications
was the key. We thought improved teamwork and organization effectiveness would follow directly from people communicating
openly with one another on matters of personal and work importance. Thus our role was clear. We identified the important issues
and brought people together to work out their differences. And
the modes we used for reconciling them ranged from sitting in as
two people discussed and argued their differing points of view, to
convening team-effectiveness meetings in which department or
division managers would get together with their boss to talk about
work unit problems and opportunities, to meeting with members
of interdepartmental task forces to help them resolve differences
and plan collaborative formats for their work together.

Our means of facilitating such events usually began with individual interviews. The purpose was to learn in advance how each participant viewed the situation in order to familiarize ourselves with the issues and personalities involved. Initially we were surprised at how much managers looked forward to these individual sessions. Later on, we discovered managers considered them more than just a chance to clarify their thinking; they saw these sessions as an insurance policy—now there was at least one other person who understood their thinking and who could help them state their views when the dialogue heated up. Thus, a major part of our early efforts entailed learning about each person's orientation and personal reasons for holding it—that is, the subjective needs that lay behind the solutions and structures they proposed. We were neutrals relating to the personal needs of each individual, promoting openness, acting as traffic cops, orchestrating problem solving, and ensuring that people would hear out and deal with someone else's divergent point of view.

Our role promoted trust. Most people, when involved in conflicts that involve different needs for structure, wind up focusing on the other person's outward behavior—the specific acts they see blocking them—and fail to recognize their compatibility with what the other person is attempting to accomplish. We can't list the number of power struggles and political moments we witnessed in which, from our vantage point, people with compatible interests were fighting without recognizing that their interests were compatible. And we can't count the number of fights we nipped in the bud simply by pointing out compatible interests and by figuring out ways for people with different procedural preferences to accommodate one another.

As we became more involved in organizations and developed better insight into people and their dilemmas in communicating, we began to see that our real impact was coming from the work we did out of the limelight, behind the scenes. Increasingly, we spent our time talking privately with people. We talked about their views of *reality*: what they perceived to be the dilemma, what organizational dynamics they believed were taking place, and what motives they thought lay behind the actions of those with whom they were relating. And, most importantly, we talked about how they needed to frame situations in order to make their points effectively. We were resources helping managers to structure the conversations they were about to have with people who were not yet in the room. Our neutrality and ability to represent a third party's interests—while empathizing with the person we were listening to—helped people search for a common meeting ground at the same time they were positioning their own interests for group acceptance.

Our writing and attempts at theoretical formulation forced us periodically to step back and reflect on the organization events we witnessed and our involvement with them. Gradually we realized that implicit in our mode of operating was a model that accounted for the sequence of actions we took in promoting improved communications—the type of communications we thought would produce organizational effectiveness. Our articulation of this model caused us to view ourselves less as clinicians and more as consciousness-raisers and perspective-setters. Certainly our skills in sizing up people and understanding their emotional needs were important. But more useful were our abilities to recognize problems caused by inadequate engagement of the subjective elements that exist regardless of the personalities involved.

We saw that our first step in enlarging people's perspectives involved getting the person we were counseling to become more conscious of how his or her own subjective interests were intertwined with what he or she advocated or opposed on behalf of the organization's effectiveness. For instance, in response to an individual's account of a brewing conflict we might say, "Oh yes, for someone with your need to be included, a 'loner' like that is a tough person to work with." With each individual we would look for opportunities to make noncritical comments aimed at heightening that person's awareness of the patterns and personal biases contained within his or her way of judging people and assessing the value of organization events.

Our second step usually involved getting people to look behind the actions of those with whom they were clashing to comprehend the subjective situation that the other person faced. We wanted people to become more conscious of the subjective framework that was determining the other person's actions and to adopt a respectful orientation to it. For instance, to a subordinate clashing with a boss, we might say, "Let's think about your boss's situation and what he's trying to do to convince *his* boss that he is exercising the proper amount of control over you." And with a boss we might say, "Yes, Tom does seem to lack focus. Now put yourself in his shoes. How do you think he sees the situation and what, in his mind, is going to constitute success?''

Our third step usually involved raising people's awareness of some aspect of the organization system and the adaptations that would be necessary for many person's needs to be met simultaneously. For instance we might ask, ''Do you have to continue the practice of giving performance reviews at the same time you review salaries?'' and then go on to explain that we see this as an organizational practice that pits a boss's needs against those needs of his or her subordinates. The boss wants a subordinate to open-mindedly critique ''self-faults'' and identify areas for self-improvement, while the subordinate wants to be seen as ''faultless'' and deserving of more pay.

In all the instances mentioned above we'd listen to the individual's account and then add in factors and dimensions that seemed important to us. As problem solvers we were always interested in the specifics but as educators we saw a more important opportunity. We sought to conduct our conversations in such a way that people would learn how to do a better job of considering subjective factors when we weren't around to help.

With our model articulated and our sequence for getting people to keep the subjective element more clearly in mind, we began to learn from what we had been looking at every day in our consulting but which, for years, we had been unable to see. And this allowed us to formulate some insights that changed our view of the organization world considerably. We realized that an individual's position of strength in an organization is as much a matter of personal *context* as it is a matter of content. By context, we mean the existence of an organizational viewpoint that highlights the value of an individual's contributions. We saw why some very able people were not valued by their organizations, and we saw why some people with mediocre abilities were highly valued. In such instances a major part of one's organizational value seemed to stem from whether or not the situation was structured in such a way that someone with that person's skills, interests, and style would be appreciated and needed. And, when we encountered people whose time seemed to have come and passed and who were experiencing dramatic changes in their organizational credibility, with no other change in their professional or managerial skills, we understood that they lacked context.

Next we saw that while few people think in terms of organizational politics, most people instinctively realize the importance of having their actions seen in the proper context and spend a good deal of energy on activities aimed at getting others to frame situations in ways that are complementary to their interests. We also saw people who put all their efforts into doing a good job—and who preferred not to get the slightest bit involved in organizational politics—arrive at a moment of truth. After a shift in organization thinking put their preferred way of seeing things out of favor with those who decide what is mainstream and valuable, they were faced with the choice of being disenfranchised, switching tacks to adopt the new point of view, or politicking to unseat the viewpoint that was now detracting from their value.

Finally, we realized how much of our own time was spent involved in organization politics. We recognized that we were *not* neutrals—we were using our presence, expertise, relationship with the boss, and insider's information to shape the backdrop realities against which subsequent organizational events would be viewed and against which people and their contributions would be valued. Of course, we thought the version of reality that we were pushing would benefit the entire organization, for we were firmly committed to finding one that would allow people with different strengths and attributes to be simultaneously valued and to have their efforts channeled so that each was organizationally relevant. We had always taken care to point out to clients that we were not in the evaluation business and that our job was to find ways for members of the current group to work more effectively together. However, we had never before realized how political our "neutral" position of saying what would benefit the entire organization was, and the vulnerability people would face if they chose to express views that opposed our brand of "objectivity."

Eventually we began to question the basis of our power and what we were doing that managers did not seem able to do for themselves. Always we realized that our effectiveness ultimately rested on our ability to teach people how to do for themselves what we were doing for them. But here we were not effective. In questioning "Why not?" it dawned on us that our methodology stemmed from a view of the organization world that contrasted sharply with the view that most managers believe and which conventional management wisdom supports. And while managers would call for our help and embrace our assistance, our way of viewing organization events eluded them. Our attempts to get across the basic assumptions which oriented us were blocked by ingrained conceptions of what organizations are.

We found that most people assume that organizations are tangible, fixed entities that exist outside of the minds that perceive them. When talking about organizations, they talk of externals and about qualities that each viewer should take at face value or at least infer from that which is readily apparent. They talk about how the job should be done, what the business plan calls for, who has a particular role, how decisions are made, what is the function of a program, how someone is valued, and so on, as if everyone who views these elements of organization should perceive them in roughly the same way. And while this way of operating allows people to be concrete and to talk objectively about organization events and their meanings, it does not go very far toward including the subjective element. It puts management in the position of telling people the meaning of organizational events rather than learning about the ways specific individuals actually view these events and the needs that underlie their views.

The assumptions that orient us are strikingly different. Our consulting and our orientation begin with a very basic point: *it is people who bring meaning to organization events rather than events possessing meanings that are revealed to those who are sufficiently objective to interpret them*. In effect, we think few organization happenings can be understood independently of understanding the minds that view them. We view organizations as entities that are essentially dependent on the needs, interests, and personal attributes of the people who comprise them. We don't think people can talk realistically about how a job should be done without also talking about the orientation of the person who has been assigned to do it. We don't think people can talk realistically about the effectiveness of a business plan or of a particular way of structuring an organization without also taking into account the unique talents, abilities, and limitations of the people who are being asked to participate in them. And we don't think it is possible to determine realistically whether a program assessment or a personnel evaluation was conducted fairly without also knowing the unique orientations and values of the people who conducted it. All of these issues can be dealt with and must, we believe, be included before a rational discussion becomes realistic.

Contrasting the assumptions we make with the ones made by the rational model led us to rethink our concept of *organization* and put it on yet more personal and subjective grounds. We see that organizations are comprised of people with diverse personal concerns and interests who, left to their own devices, are inclined to (1) interpret the same organization events differently from one another; (2) mistakenly expect that others will view these events more or less as they have viewed them; and (3) depend excessively on organizational power and power politics for reconciling these differences in views. Incidentally, most people don't think of themselves as engaging in power politics. However, the perspectives presented in this book will show that this is, in fact, very often the case.

On the other hand, we believe that organizational effectiveness depends on the extent to which people who work together are able to reconcile their personal differences in perception and expectation without resorting to power politics. We think that an *effective organization* is one in which people possess the same overarching objective(s), recognize and respect personal differences in perception, and see and interpret events related to their common objective(s) in roughly the same or compatible ways. Conversely, we think that an *ineffective organization* is a group of people, oftentimes with the same overarching objective, who see and interpret events differently and lack the means for reconciling their differences. And we think *disorganization* leading to chaos is an extreme form of ineffective organization where people not only have areas of incompatibility they can not reconcile but operate in ways that are basically disrespectful of the other person's right to view events differently.

Thus, an effective organization depends on people (with comparable goals) possessing the relationships and communication processes to deal constructively with their personal differences. And *good communication* does not merely entail people telling one another what they want. It entails people telling one another enough about themselves and the needs that lie behind what they want so that others can better understand how they see events, what they hope to achieve, and why they are proceeding in a specific way. Good communications entails people exchanging what needs to be exchanged so that they will better understand the meanings that others are likely to assign to the next organizational event in which they jointly participate.

These perspectives have allowed us to be more precise about the managerial practices that produce effective organizations and about our consulting goals. Managers need to spend more time comprehending subjective interests and dealing more directly with the roles specific individuals play in determining their unit's goals, processes, and basic perceptions. The consultant's role in facilitating good communications and effective organization is to coach managers on how to help people with different ways of interpreting meaning, different modes of operating effectively, and different needs for success to see one another more accurately and to find ways of complementing one another. In the course of daily operations many naturally competitive moments occur. Without attention to good communications and effective organization these moments produce the power struggles that can threaten anyone's hopes for success and general well-being.

We have chosen the term "radical management" to indicate that fundamental change in the perspectives managers use at work is needed. And for our purpose it is interesting to note that *radical* is a word with two meanings. It means "a sharp departure from the past" and it means "a return to the root and that which is basic and fundamental." For us, returning to the root means accepting that the individual is the basic unit of organization. Many people already espouse a similar rhetoric in making such statements as "people are our most important resource." However, few such pronouncements say enough about the nature of people and their subjective interests to make them more than slogans. In this book we present a model of the individual and his or her personal needs and organizational commitments and describe departures from present overly rationalistic practices that allow management to actually engage the subjective element more effectively.

In advocating departures from present practices, we do not intend this to be a "how to" book with prescriptions that translate directly into action. We do, however, intend it to be a *"how to comprehend"* book with perspectives that reorient managerial practices. Our overriding goal is to provide managers and professionals with a more accurate map of the organizational dynamics transpiring around them, particularly with respect to expression of the subjective element. We also provide models aimed at helping people see new options and exercise more choice. Ultimately, new perspectives must be applied to the specific situation an individual faces, and integrated with each person's unique contribution. We feel our views readily lend themselves to such individualized incorporation.

Overview

This book is presented in five sections. Section I provides insight into the role subjective forces play in shaping the lives and fortunes of people at work. The elements and dynamics of trust and politics are explained to give readers a deeper sense of what is required to achieve trusting relationships, and of the forces opposing their creation. Section II shifts attention to the role subjective forces play in shaping the political realities that determine organizational directions and the power plays that take place among people who seek personally convenient modifications to these directions. Section III presents models that allow managers to develop insight into the subjective commitments of others and to be strategic in their dealings with them. Taken as a package, these three sections contain the basic framework of our "radical" perspective. They demonstrate how the reality of an organization is as much determined by internal politics as it is by market forces, and they show how to comprehend with accuracy the unique intent behind a specific individual's participation.

Section IV is our "applications" section. It contains novel perspectives on team-building, leadership, motivation, and power aimed at helping people transcend their overly rationalistic training in management. Our radical approach requires that people take explicit account of the subjective element or risk being overwhelmed by what they fail to acknowledge. The Conclusion takes a sober look at the cost of continued reliance on the rational model and specifies the shifts in perspective needed to operate differently.

SECTION I

The Pursuit of Trust

CHAPTER 2

Context, Politics, and Trusting Relationships

In our work as consultants, we see managers spending more and more time promoting trust and emphasizing the importance of trusting relationships. To us this makes perfect sense, for we've long contended that the trusting relationship is the most efficient management tool ever invented. We know of no other management device that saves more time or promotes more organizational effectiveness. Trusting relationships make a flawed organizational plan work. Trusting relationships provide the key to good communications, create the conditions for teamwork, rectify badly timed actions, and soften the impact of otherwise slanderous and explosive communications. In short, trusting relationships create the conditions for organization success.

Conversely, nothing can erode organizational effectiveness more quickly than a relationship that lacks trust. Without trust, everyday misunderstandings are taken as betrayals; simple directives become strident expressions; the best conceived plans fail. Without trust, individuals overpersonalize criticism and seek to hide the weak spots in their performance. Without trust, communications become wordy and defensive as individuals fight on issues that need to be open-mindedly discussed if the organization is to be effective. Without trust, risk taking, innovation, and creativity are stifled as individuals place "not making a mistake" ahead of seeking out new opportunities and taking chances. And, without trust, too many decisions focus on short-term tangible results as the pressures to justify today's performance squeeze out actions that invest in tomorrow's capacity.

Unfortunately, our work has shown us that trusting relationships are becoming more and more difficult to produce. We see too many managers caught up in the rational model, mistaking the rhetoric of teamwork for actual trust and real cooperation. Every manager and every organization has the words, slogans, and surface actions to convey the image of a work unit as a "team," and most have the desire to make it one, but in our estimation relatively few are involved in the real thing.

The problem is understandable. The overly rational mind-set produces misconceptions of what trust entails. *First*, people mistake the desire for teamwork and the commitment to abstract virtues such as openness, honesty, and integrity for trust-building skills. They believe that their sincerity and collaborative spirit will be recognized by others whom they expect to respond in kind. But when people encounter someone caught up in a manipulative moment, they are inclined to react to that person's manipulation as a violation of team spirit and a justification for abandoning their own commitment to the aforementioned virtues.

Second, most people underestimate the everyday nature of organizational politics and fail to realize that many actions that seem organizationally constructive to them will meet with opposition from someone else. They underestimate how political their actions and justifications appear to others with different motives. The result is an organization world in which almost everyone claims to eschew organization politics, engages in activities that others see as political, and fails to understand why what seems reasonable and logical to him or her appears to others to be politically motivated. And the rhetoric that says teamwork and trust are taking place when they are not confuses matters all the more.

A *third* misconception people have about what trust entails rests in the belief that trust is "objectively" related to something another person does and, in particular, to that person's ability to perform competently. We often hear people say something like "I trust him because I can count on him to do a good job." But we've seen too many instances of people who appear competent being trusted by one person and not by a second, and of people denying someone's trustworthiness despite significant data and testimonials to the contrary, for us to deny that subjective and political considerations play a major role in determining whether or not someone is judged competent.

Our interest in an alternative to rational management takes on a tangible form when we observe the difficult time managers have producing trust. Perhaps more than any key ingredient to organization effectiveness, trust symbolizes the importance and centrality of the subjective element. As a consequence, examining it enables us to take a closer look at the range and intensity of the subjective forces that shape organizational life.

For an illustration of the trust difficulties the rationalistic orientation can produce, consider an up-and-coming manager named Mark, who found himself in a fix which prompted him to call upon us for advice. Mark said he needed help in sorting out his relationship with a subordinate who was giving him a difficult time. We had worked with Mark earlier in his career, and his energy and abilities had long ago won our respect.

Mark had taken over as corporate planning director a year earlier and, from the outset, had been unhappy with the performance of a key staff member named Larry. Mark said his main job was to get line management more involved in the actual planning process and that, in the face of this effort, Larry had been nothing but dead weight. Larry appeared to be so caught up in perfecting the mechanics of planning that he couldn't find the time to teach line management how to apply them. In Mark's mind Larry was just one of those individuals who, to operate effectively, needed high levels of structure and certainty. The concept of taking planning tools to managers, rather than doing the planning for them, seemed to overwhelm Larry. Mark said he had tried hard to give Larry clues about the modified orientation he expected from him but, by the time Larry's formal performance review session rolled around four months later, he had given up. Mark had concluded that his and Larry's orientations didn't match up and he felt compelled to tell Larry as much.

Mark's attempt to level with Larry went badly. In the face-to-face review session Mark stated his concerns candidly. In response, Larry said he had been working hard to please Mark and felt good about his performance. And when Larry had asked for specific suggestions for improvement, Mark bluntly told him that, given the fluid nature of the job, Larry was too much in need of structure and that both of them would be better off if a "transfer" were arranged.

Mark said he was shocked when Larry refused to leave his department and, instead, sought support from two previous planning directors, each of whom now held big jobs in the corporation. Both of these men had previously given superior performance reviews to Larry and were sufficiently distressed to visit Mark and express their concerns that personal differences might cost the company an extremely competent and valuable employee. Both made the point that there was nothing wrong with Larry's mode of planning and that, for over five years, it had served the company well. Mark told us, "With this type of support for Larry, I had no choice but to back down and try to make the best of the situation." At the end of his first year, however, Mark realized that the relationship lacked any semblance of trust and, desperate for help, sought our consultation.

More important than the help we delivered is the fact that Mark's fix illustrates some of the classic blind spots in rational management. To begin with, up until the time Larry's former bosses got involved, Mark was proceeding with almost no recognition of the extent to which his own subjective preferences were determining his vision of what constituted effective planning. As a man on the way up, Mark's instinct was to identify areas where he could make a distinctive contribution. After all, Mark wasn't going to make much of a name for himself by being known only as a person who could effectively operate what other directors had created previously. However, out of proportion in the opportunity Mark saw for himself was his belief that any continuation of existing ways would constitute an organizational deficit.

By not explicitly acknowledging the subjective biases that underlie their commitments and preferred modes of operating, managers often have a difficult time communicating basic expectations. Certainly Mark had never given Larry a clear message of what he wanted from him. There was poor Larry, knocking himself out, trying to do what he thought Mark wanted, only to find out that he was being perceived as rigidly pursuing "obsolete" goals. And, of course, Mark also was shocked and surprised to discover that what he saw as incompetence was actually a monumental effort to please him.

The rationalistic model leads managers like Mark to operate without sufficient appreciation for the amount and range of differences that actually exist among people at work. It's true that Larry's work relied heavily on structured approaches; in fact, his ability to structure planning activities so that line managers didn't have to spend excessive time performing them was a major reason why former bosses rated him so highly. But when Mark sensed that Larry wasn't meeting his expectations he failed to consider the possibility that it was Larry's style that bothered him, not Larry's results.

The rationalistic model leads managers who are not getting the subordinate performance they want to dig big holes for themselves. Problems of missed expectations are defined as subordinate deficiencies with focus on the shortcomings and flaws of the person who performed "inadequately." The problem in this way of operating is that it leaves one little choice but to dispose of the "flawed" human. Mark confided that once he locked into a definition of the problem that blamed Larry for his inability to operate in low structure situations, such as consulting with line management, there were times when even he observed himself moving precipitously to fire Larry. In the months following the performance appraisal Mark had come to appreciate Larry's value but knew no way to convince Larry of this. After all that had transpired, Larry wouldn't trust him.

The tendency to make subjective judgments about an individual's competence or incompetence based on the compatibility of that person's skills and basic orientation with one's own is well recognized within management. Nevertheless, whenever we isolate an instance of an apparently competent individual being valued by one person and not by a second, we ask ourselves, "What else is involved?" And in most instances we find that the "What else" pertains to whether or not the evaluator believes the person he or she is judging is inclined to appreciate his or her different orientation and express support for it in public settings. For instance, highly organized people are inclined to value and trust others who are organized and are willing to endorse the benefits of that approach in public. Conversely, people are disinclined to value those who don't comprehend their unique ways of being competent or whom they perceive to be in situations in which that person's way of being competent will compete with their own. For instance, a "thinking" type may distrust an action-oriented type and fear that that individual's propensity for action will cause him or her to undervalue someone who is more analytic and whose "actions" do not produce immediate results.

In sizing up whether or not one individual is inclined to give a generous interpretation to the skills and actions of a second, we often ask "Is that person getting the half-full or the half-empty water glass treatment?" Using the terms half-full and half-empty is our shorthand way of asking whether one is being evaluated in the context of what is in his or her "container of competencies" or by what is missing. People trust those who they feel are looking to recognize their strengths and to understand how they might be maximally effective. And, people trust those who they believe recognize their imperfections and areas of lesser competence and are looking to help them structure situations so that these imperfections do not become important weaknesses. *Trust, then, is a quality people extend to those who appear to offer them basic support and who seem to value their ways of contributing to the organization's effectiveness.*

As we have described, whether or not one individual is inclined to relate positively to another person's strengths, value his or her goals, comprehend the reasons for his or her actions, recognize specific abilities, or favorably view his or her imperfections depends, to a large extent, on how that first person perceives his or her own orientation and its compatibility with that of the other person. Competitive forces, such as those alluded to above, can make it difficult to cast another in a positive light at moments when that second person's orientation appears to create obstacles for the first person's success. In the rational model, internal competition is healthy because it is a force promoting excellence. In the subjective model, internal competition can be unhealthy. It can provide people with reasons for not relating to the strengths that an associate brings to his or her job, and for finding covert ways to diminish another person's role and contributions. We have great concern about the ability of contemporary management to make accurate discriminations between healthy and unhealthy competition and this is an issue we take up repeatedly throughout this book.

Thus, at their roots, trust and trusting relationships have large personal, subjective, and political components. Competence plays a part, but it too is dependent on whether a viewer has an orientation that allows him or her to see a second person's strengths and to acknowledge these strengths in a particular organizational situation. What's more, most of the people who populate organizations are imperfect performers and whether or not they are viewed as competent depends totally on the situation in which they are expected to perform. People who are competent in one situation, with one set of viewer expectations, are not necessarily competent in the next. For example, consider the following discussion held by two senior managers, and the consequences attached to setting someone's expectations straight.

MANAGER 1: I had lunch with that new trainee in the Dallas plant last Tuesday. I definitely was *not* impressed.

MANAGER 2: Never met him myself but we need him as a production management backup.

MANAGER 1: Oh production! That makes sense. I couldn't place him in general management.

MANAGER 2: Perhaps someday he'll make general management but right now I hear he's doing an outstanding job where he is.

MANAGER 1: Now that you put it that way, I agree.

The above example brings us to the point where we can use the word that is foremost in our minds when we think of trust and what constitutes the basis of a trusting relationship. That word is "context." People trust those who have the ability to view them in the proper "context" and who have the inclination to use and respect that context at moments when self-interests and job orientations place them in competition. Once one accepts the importance of the personal, subjective, and political components of organization life, one then realizes that in an organization few behaviors stand on their own—most require an interpretation—and context is a word that characterizes the frame of reference that underlies any particular interpretation.

Being viewed in the proper context—the frame of reference that accurately reflects what an individual had in mind when taking an action—and having that frame of reference accepted as organizationally valuable makes all the difference in one's organizational reading. In fact we go so far as to assert that *context is the root of an individual's organizational power*. Context is the difference between being viewed as an overly gregarious engineer who is no longer a technically creative R&D performer and as an engineer who has the technical know-how to head "Customer Relations" and just the right personality to go along with it. Context is the difference between being seen as an individual who gets paid too much for an easy job and an individual with outstanding aptitudes and competencies who is "learning the ropes," and is temporarily in a situation that doesn't allow him or her to use very many of his or her skills and talents.

In an organization people and groups operate with different responsibilities and different personal orientations and hence acquire different needs for context. However, exactly which frame of reference might be most appropriately applied is not self-evident to one's organizational colleagues. And, left to their own devices, people are inclined to view another person's or another group's effects from the frame of reference that applies to their own set of commitments. For example, recently we were called in to help with a huge flap created by a vice-president who had flown in his regional managers for three days of meetings. The senior executives questioned whether this expense constituted a good use of company resources during a period of budget cuts and low profitability. The executives lacked the context for seeing value in such a meeting and thought the main message regarding stricter fiduciary controls could be handled in a conference telephone call and less important topics by an exchange of written correspondence. We heard comments like: "You had to fly all those people to New York?"; "To talk about what?"; "And all you heard were reports you could have read?"; "And some also brought their wives?—Now you've got to be kidding!"

These statements came from people who could not relate to the role the meeting was intended to play in this management team's development, nor to the opportunities created for informal give and take on a highly sensitive issue that the vice-president did not want listed on the formal agenda, nor to the alarm that might have been created by canceling a regularly scheduled management committee meeting because of a cash problem that this same management was calling "temporary." Context is something over which people often conflict. It's something everyone needs. Without it a person becomes instantly vulnerable, but when one has it, it makes a person feel very powerful.

In an organization, every behavior, every act and effort, is open to someone else's critique. Almost any accomplishment can be picked apart. Everyone's and every group's story can be contested and even destroyed. Any or all of this happens when a person whose opinion counts uses the "wrong" context in sizing up or evaluating what is taking place. Within the "wrong" context even an outstanding effort can easily be judged to be inadequate. Of course by "wrong" we mean a context produced by expectations that differ from what the person performing a given behavior, or the group taking a certain action had in mind when acting the way he, she, or they did.

Someone who is viewed in the "wrong" context will seldom be accorded full appreciation for his or her individual skills, role, and value. Almost always the result is a diminishment—a diminishment of the value of what was attempted and a diminishment in the value of what was accomplished. And, in any large organization, being viewed in the "wrong" context, in a framework that diminishes what one is about, constitutes a loss of power.

When people feel their positive efforts are unappreciated, three questions need to be asked. First, "Are they viewing me in the proper context?" Second, "Can they be motivated to search for a more proper one?" Third, "Will they deal respectfully with my way of contributing at moments when they view it as competitive with their own?" In large organizations, one is often viewed by people who lack the proper context and who lack the motivation to search for it. In such instances, trusting relationships are not possible. On the other hand, an association with someone who is not viewing one in the proper context but who genuinely desires to do so, presents a wonderful beginning for a potentially trusting relationship.

Trust relates to one's confidence that someone else has the motivation to view his or her behavior in the context of what he or she actually meant to accomplish and to respect it. "Does this person see the connection between what I'm doing and what the organization needs to have accomplished?" "When he doesn't understand, will he ask me the reasons behind what I'm doing or will he automatically assume that my goals were the same as his and that in terms of these goals my actions make little sense?" "Will she give the half-full or half-empty interpretation to what I've done?" "How will he treat the flaws in my performance?" These are the types of questions that should race through a person's mind when deciding whether or not to trust someone.

In an organization, a trusting relationship is based on the belief that a second person will make an earnest attempt to view one's behavior within the context of what one had in mind when acting in a certain way. That is, the second person will attempt to relate not only to one's behavior but also to the intentions and perspective that produced it. A trusting relationship is also based on the belief that this second person will take a supportive stance toward one's flawed performances—toward those instances where one's behavior does not successfully accomplish what one set out to create. This does not mean that two people enter a pact whereby they mutually agree to fudge reality to portray the other's deeds in an overly positive light. It means that they form a supportive relationship aimed at understanding the problems the other is having in putting his or her viewpoint across. In doing so, the second person may choose to withhold expressing his or her opposing views. But the expectation is that later on, when the time is right, the second person will raise those differing opinions for the first person's consideration. A trusting relationship ought to be sufficiently robust that participants can challenge one another to consider the other contexts or frames of reference in which their actions are being seen. Of course this robust quality comes from each participant's knowledge that the other sees where he or she is coming from as a viable orientation.

Trusting relationships get people through the rough spots in their organizational dealings. Knowing that associates are looking to identify the context that accurately reflects one's intentions can give an individual a feeling of power and the confidence to perform his or her best. Then one can concentrate on what he or she is doing and avoid the distractions that come from worrying about how his or her actions are being read. When people lack confidence that others are motivated to put them in the proper context, they necessarily divert energy from what they are doing and focus it on getting others to take a receptive point of view—they play politics. In doing so, their performance suffers from distraction and they lose their flexibility.

Being seen in the proper context is the key to a trusting relationship. On the other hand, not being seen in the proper context and having to relate to people one does not trust intensifies one's needs to achieve context. Lacking context, but needing it in order to have one's efforts valued, drives people to extremes. This is exactly what people tell us about when they say that they are battling with someone else. It's a struggle for context that produces the type of power politics that most people associate with organizational fighting. People feel their well-being and security threatened, and this produces the need to achieve a more proper context, even if doing so involves the use of artificial and fraudulent means. They then resort to behind-the-scenes tactics aimed at forcing others to give them a friendly reading or at least to go along with them publicly. They frame events manipulatively to emphasize what they want others to conclude; they give fragmented versions of what they know to be the truth to feature that version which gets them what they want; and, they play it both ways by giving others the impression that they are in general agreement when actually they are not.

Now we have gone full circle. Trusting relationships are essential to an organization's effectiveness. Context is essential to each individual's effectiveness. People trust those who have the ability and the inclination to view them in the proper context and distrust those who don't. What's more, people don't take the deprivation of context lying down; they fight back. They use power politics to manipulate reality in attempts to force others either to view them in the proper context or to go along with them in public. And to the extent that context is difficult to come by in an organization, everyone has a problem. Those in charge of the organization have a problem. Those who lack it have a problem. And, ironically, even those who have context have a problem. Their situations are unstable since others, who lack power because they have not yet achieved sufficient context, will be looking for every opportunity to take it, which often means at their expense.

CHAPTER 3

Why People Engage in Organization Politics

Along with trust, organization politics is the topic that comes up most often when we talk subjectivity with managers. It's a topic about which a majority of managers feel extremely ambivalent and are on record in claiming they wish it would go away. Managers are adamant about politics; they deeply resent their involvement, believe their involvement is caused by *someone else's* actions, and are frustrated by their inability to withstand getting swept up in the fray.

In our discussions, most managers treat politics as a "black box" with contents they know very little about. By and large the questions they raise are aimed at symptomatic relief. At the junior and middle levels, where most managers are interested in developing the skills required to climb the hierarchy, the majority of the questions concern surviving a specific situation that is perceived to be politically dangerous. Occasionally the discussion extends to getting the jump on the next situation by learning how to spot the presence of political forces and to take action that guarantees that one's actions are perceived "positively." At the senior levels, where many managers feel responsibility for the health and well-being of the system, we get questions concerning the extent and nature of this "peril" to efficiency within the ranks. They ask what can be done to help others spend more time doing their jobs and less time maneuvering and worrying about how they are being perceived. We hear such questions as "How necessary and pervasive are politics and what purpose do they serve?" and "Are some modes of political behavior more organizationally constructive than others and, if so, what can we do to insure that they take the more constructive form here?"

To us, questions like these present marvelous opportunities to educate, for their answers link the basic elements of subjectivity to what is fundamental in creating an effective organization. Usually these questions are asked by managers with pressing problems who, failing to get symptomatic relief, are ready to tackle the underlying issues. Of course the phenomena these questions focus on are complex and for this reason we like to discuss them one issue at a time.

How Necessary and Pervasive Are Politics and What Purpose Do They Serve?

In our organization travels we are constantly confronted with the mystique associated with organization politics and with people's fascination for the political moment. Apparently managers see politics as a key element in the process of attaining power, for their eyes always seem to be scanning for anecdotes and incidents on which they can school themselves. For instance, consider the reflections of an up-and-coming manager when circumstances presented him with an insider's view of a situation he deemed political.

"I didn't really know Chuck before we flew east together to attend a meeting of the corporate management committee. We spent five hours together talking nonstop. It was particularly informative to hear how someone new to our company at the vice-presidential level sized up our computer operation. Everyone thinks it's been running out of control for years. All that experience in public accounting sure gives him an interesting point of view.

The fascinating part was watching him in the meeting. I knew he had been brought in to reevaluate our decentralization policy and to recommend changes aimed at giving headquarters more control. From our conversation I learned that he was engaging some of our heavyweights for the first time and that he had already drawn some strong conclusions. What's more, it was immediately apparent that he thinks differently than the rest of them.

Well, that was an exercise in maneuvering. Chuck's a real politician. He sure knows how to handle himself. I understood that with a mandate like his Chuck has to be very careful not to alienate the very people whose cooperation will be key to implementing whatever change he might eventually propose. On the other hand, I could see that he also needed to show enough of what he was thinking to scare the division managers a bit and prevent them from believing that they could hold him and his reforms off indefinitely.

On only a few occasions did Chuck assert himself directly. And when he did the others became noticeably uncomfortable. You should have seen them! Grown men and women tripped all over themselves attempting to give the impression that they would agree with Chuck if only he would yield on a few minor issues. But from my conversation with Chuck, I could see that the small concessions they wanted him to make were basic points in where he was heading.

For his part, Chuck was magnificent. He picked his spots carefully and most of the time confined himself to asking questions that drew a distinction between his point of view and theirs. He subtly put down the importance of ideas he opposed by taking pains to back up his assertions with the rules of 'good' professionalism and practices that had yielded tangible results in successful operations elsewhere. Only once did he let it really hang out. That was in a ten-minute blast in which he said, 'I know operation audits have been done differently for years. But if I have the responsibility to insure their accuracy then I have to do things the way they make sense to me.' Then he proceeded to lay out his methodology, implying that anyone who thought differently was behind the times. But most of the time he smiled and nodded thoughtfully and gave all the external appearances of getting along. And with those who got emotional he was quick to schedule a breakfast or a lunch in an attempt to establish more rapport.

It was a couple of days into the meetings when Chuck and I wound up at the bar alone having an after-dinner drink. I was feeling kind of loose and couldn't resist letting him know that I understood. So I said, 'Chuck, you're a master politician' and complimented him on the way he dominated the meeting.

Well, talk about rubbing someone the wrong way; he hit the
ceiling. Later on he apologized but made it abundantly clear
that any further attempt to label his behavior 'political' would
jeopardize our relationship. Then he threw his arm around me
and said he appreciated our friendship and that I was a clever
fellow myself.''

Were Chuck's actions political? In our view they were, because
they were directed towards changing the way others related to organization events with the goals of creating context and power for
himself. They were political because the images Chuck was pushing involved motives that were not always apparent to those who
were affected by them.

Were Chuck's actions necessary? They certainly seem to have
been. Chuck's mandate to centralize certain functions would deprive others of a degree of autonomy they preferred not to relin-
quish. Moreover, being aboveboard and direct in stating his objective would probably produce more resistance than he could
successfully oppose using logic alone. Of course he could always
assert that he was merely doing what higher-ups wanted to have
accomplished, but that would discredit his independence and deprive him of the opportunity to develop people's confidence. Instead Chuck sought a political process aimed at gradually creating
a line of reasoning that others would accept as justification for
tightening headquarters' control. In the process, Chuck could establish himself as a reasonable person whom others might grow to
trust.

How extraordinary was Chuck's behavior, and did he set out to
be political? To us, behavior like Chuck's is a common everyday
occurrence which, in one form or another, we'd speculate everybody at that meeting was engaged in. Probably no one, including
Chuck, had it in his or her own mind to be political, and that
would be ironic, since the concept of centralization was well
known to be controversial. To us, all this is understandable since
politics is the source of many organizational ironies. People do not
intend to act politically, yet they are constantly finding themselves
in work situations where the forces bearing on them evoke a political response. People seldom see themselves acting politically, yet
almost everyone recognizes such actions by others. People don't
often see how what takes place out front creates the need for a
behind-the-scenes response, yet almost everyone sees the need to

work behind the scenes to create more appreciation for themselves and more understanding for their point of view.

As we said, when it comes to organization politics most managers have limited views. They are unhappy about the presence of politics in their own organization and curtail their thinking to circumscribed episodes. When asked about politics they describe specific incidents such as shootouts at the top, injustices in which someone got promoted ahead of a more deserving individual, personal disappointments in which they lost out on something they wanted, and competitive moments in which someone gained the upper hand in a situation that ought to have been determined more fairly. Most cite examples where politics were initiated by someone using deceptive and sometimes destructive practices to circumvent the system for self-interested gain. Usually their accounts feature costs to the organization, success at someone else's expense, and alliances that yield reciprocal gain. And behind all of these accounts is the notion that competition exists among people who, from the standpoint of the organization's interests, ought to be collaborating.

Some managers extend their thinking about politics to include instances where a team, group, or entire organization fashioned an appeal to meet the interests of another group and, because of their political sensitivity, were able to outsmart the competition and gain special advantage. In the same vein, some people cite examples of political blunders such as the time when, only a few days after squeezing auto union workers for benefit concessions and cutbacks in pay, General Motors executives announced that they had voted themselves a significant raise in salary.

All of this thinking about politics makes good sense but, to us, reflects a line of reasoning that does not go far enough. It focuses on the acts of politics but not the cause. It focuses on the calculated and indirect ways people promote themselves and their projects but does not explain why people feel they can't promote what they believe in more directly and still succeed. And because so many of the acts that most people recognize as political have a behind-the-scenes manipulative character, with the perpetrator's real intentions hidden from the view of those he or she is attempting to influence, people's references to politics almost always carry a devious connotation and are viewed as organizational negatives.

The view that politics is devious and represents an organizational negative offers very little in the practical sense. Politics exists and that's a fact. It is part and parcel of the business affairs of the people one cheers for as well as of those one labels as villains. Oh, there are forms of politics one feels better about: those that utilize less deception and less conscious manipulation and those that present an honest portrayal of reality as the individual knows it. But even with these portrayals, one gets into philosophical questions such as how much *tailoring* of the truth (one can't tell everything) represents a manipulation, and whether an honest portrayal (as the individual knows it) necessarily makes one's account valid for people with different needs and interests.

The inadequacies of most people's understanding about politics are perhaps best illustrated by what most people think are the goals of organizational politics. Most familiar are thoughts of others trying to short-circuit the system for personal gain, often at the expense of someone else, or selfishly trying to push their group's projects ahead at a cost of a net gain to the overall system. However, from our experience, we find that these are not the most common goals of politics and, in fact, most of the political incidents that we identify are not so nefariously self-centered—they are ordinary acts engaged in by people with the best of intentions. Their intentions are to gain context.

Thus to our way of seeing things, the most common goal of politics is the individual's need for *context*—the need to have events viewed in a way that causes one's efforts to make organizational sense. Acts of politics include any action an individual takes in the service of creating context either for him- or herself or for a point of view to which he or she is committed. Politics, then, entails promoting acceptance for a frame of reference that gets one's actions, viewpoints, and/or contributions seen, understood, and valued.

In our minds the issue is clear; *organization politics*—the self-interested structuring of reality to gain context—is a given in any situation and those who are smart always take this into account. And from our perspective, most political acts are constructive in their intent; they are aimed at establishing the conditions needed for an individual to operate effectively. However, while the intent is constructive, too many context-seeking actions are not constructive. In fact, on-line, relatively few people understand that they are really seeking context and, from the organization's standpoint, they act destructively. They put tremendous energy into structuring reality, attempting to control how others view events, without much concern for the personal effectiveness needs of these others.

What's more, they fail to recognize the everyday nature and magnitude of their political involvements.

Lack of insight into the political ramifications of their behavior causes most people to act in ways that make trusting relationships difficult to attain. They go about establishing context without giving much conscious consideration to the fact that others hear them telling self-serving versions of the truth and without much insight into what the other person needs in the way of context in order to see him or her as organizationally effective. Trusting relationships depend on people displaying empathy for the unique frame of reference that someone else uses to view organization events. Unfortunately, the self-centered political acts in which most people engage, in the service of establishing their own context, fail to evoke such empathy.

Are Some Modes of Political Behavior More Organizationally Constructive Than Others?

We have carefully observed how people attempt to gain context in order to see the orientations they use and what earns them trusting relationships. We have seen people engage others with two distinct orientations—one we call *tactical*, the other *strategic*. In the "tactical" orientation the individual is focused on his or her own needs for context and takes little responsibility for the fact that others always have at least somewhat different needs. In the "strategic" orientation, the individual pursues his or her needs for context, acknowledges that others have different needs, and takes responsibility for the fact that the organization's effectiveness depends on the extent to which everyone's needs for context are satisfied.

We call the first orientation "tactical" because, when using it, an individual seems to monitor each moment and each event for the opportunity it holds to advance elements of his or her preferred context and generally to get the situation defined in ways that are compatible with his or her self-interested pursuits. It's the orientation that most people use most of the time because it is the quickest way to insure oneself of context. Using the tactical orientation, people relate to someone else's words and actions primarily from the standpoint of learning what specific appeal for context will be effective and how they might get that other person to go along with their own preferred way of seeing things. Unfortunately, the tactical mode of operation creates context at the expense of trusting relationships. It places one in competition with the very people with whom one is attempting to develop feelings of empathy and mutual support.

The second orientation is one that only a few people are able to use with any consistency. We call it "strategic" because its use by people who have the capacity to establish trusting relationships creates the attitude and respect that motivate others to want to put the user, and his or her pursuits, in the proper context. When using a strategic orientation, a person seeks context through a relationship in which he or she strives to understand where another individual is coming from and what the individual is attempting to accomplish both organizationally and personally, and generally makes that other individual's needs for context part of his or her own organizational concerns.

Most people would prefer to orient strategically but find that if they lack the organizational power to insist that others respond in kind, doing so makes them excessively dependent on the good will, self-discipline, and sacrifice of others. In today's organizational world, it takes a great deal of effort and skill for someone to maintain a focus on another person's needs while simultaneously pursuing his or her own. And, if others don't respond in kind, diverting focus to the needs of others merely lessens one's own chances of accomplishing what one sincerely believes is organizationally correct with no offsetting gains to compensate. Thus most people have a dilemma. They see themselves as too organizationally weak to use the strategic orientation, not strong enough to forego the tactical, and live their organization lives feeling unappreciated for the sacrifice and teamwork they would willingly contribute if only they could do so without jeopardizing their own organizational image and the security that goes along with it.

The Tactical Orientation

As we said, most people use a tactical orientation most of the time. It is often the only orientation that makes practical sense. The organization world presents a competitive environment and the people who succeed are the ones who are successful in getting external situations defined in ways that fit with their own needs for context. For example, whether a pitch for a new marketing concept requires a position paper or a verbal presentation depends on the marketing manager's ability to present his or her thoughts convincingly one way or another. All things being equal, people choose the modalities that best correspond to their strengths, values, and interests and then find organizationally sound reasons to justify what they are doing.

It is important to stress that we do not condemn the tactical approach out of hand; it is often the only way to be effective. What's more, many see it as the only expedient way of transacting with people who don't matter that much in the ongoing course of one's organizational life. After all, it's not possible to form relationships with everyone with whom one must communicate. Our concern, however, lies with our observation that most people do not understand the longer-term consequences of operating tactically and many do not see a viable alternative.

At the individual level, the problem lies in the ease with which a tactical orientation can become a way of life that is self-perpetuating. In the process of structuring and reconstructing events to fit in with one's personal needs and circumstances, an individual creates an ever-expanding need to be even more tactical in the next instant, especially when facing those whom he or she outsmarted the last time around. What's more, in being tactical, the individual derives short-term leverage from promoting logics that have power for the moment but fail to provide others with essential information: others do not get an accurate picture of what the individual is trying to achieve or why a particular approach fits in with his or her own personal brand of effectiveness. The result is that others cannot put that individual in the proper context, nor do they develop the incentive to do so. Again, trusting relationships are not forthcoming.

When we thought about examples to illustrate tactical orientations, the types of relationships they beget, and how they become a way of life, two managers, Barry and Alvin, instantly came to mind. Coincidentally their stories intertwine.

Barry is as nice a man as you'd ever want to meet. He's not well educated, but he's bright and he works in an industry where very few hold college degrees. His goal in life is quite simple: to climb as high in the corporate structure as he can.

When we first met Barry he had a background in accounting and was in the final month of a three-year assignment as assistant to his corporation's president. The last few years had been a period of aggressive expansion and Barry saw and learned a great deal by sitting in numerous meetings where potential plant acquisitions were discussed, decisions were made, and managers of acquired firms were critiqued and, more often than not, replaced.

When the question of Barry's next assignment came up he asked to be made a plant manager. He had his mind set on becoming a line vice-president and accurately perceived that in this company almost no one made it to the V.P. level without the experience of running a plant. Barry's request came as a real surprise to top management, who scoffed at first because he had no previous plant experience. His only operating knowledge came from doing research on companies that were candidates for acquisition and sitting in while executives discussed what his data meant. However, once the corporate president had a chance to think about Barry's request he became more sympathetic. After all, one couldn't quarrel with Barry's desire to add operating experience to his record. Having both corporate staff and line experiences would really establish his credentials for promotion. So, because he liked Barry and thought him quite able, the president countered with the proposal that a one-year training program leading to "consideration" for a plant manager's job be set up; Barry could learn the rudiments without excessive risk to the company or his own career. He even agreed that Barry could keep his current salary which was two thousand dollars more than most plant managers earn before their bonus when they make one.

Barry countered with, "That seems like a lot of training with no guarantees. Trim the training down to six months, guarantee me a plant, and I'll take it." Other corporate executives balked, and while the issue was being reconsidered a key directorship became available in the accounting department. It paid more, came with a car, and Barry thought would, as a next step, lead to a staff vice-presidency. This opening gave those who had reluctantly endorsed the president's proposal a chance to express more of their reservations about Barry's ability to make it in operations, and they saw his taking the accounting job as an opportunity to fill a major vacancy problem immediately. They urged Barry to accept and he did.

Within three months of Barry's taking the accounting job a second accounting director was hired. This man came with all the credentials Barry lacked. He had a college degree and was a CPA. What's more, he had technical savvy and was recognized as someone who could further professionalize the accounting staff. For Barry the handwriting was on the wall. In order to be promoted he would have to move on.

About this time a vice-president named Alvin was brought in from the field and given responsibility for all field operations. Talk about your hard-nosed, street-fighting managers, Alvin is one of the toughest. Behind his back he was called "a shark" and corporate executives chuckled when discussing the measures Alvin would take to restore order to operations. We knew Alvin when he was in the field and had seen him work. He usually got his way but at the other guy's expense. If people didn't agree with him he would say they were wrong and then go about reinterpreting organizational events to prove his point. Alvin had a knack for saying "I made a mistake, I thought Ken could handle it," while the "Kens" buckled under pressure and lost their jobs.

Alvin's mode of operating was relatively simple and, on the surface, almost pleasant. He'd go into a plant, explore what was wrong, and then ask for a remedy and a timetable. Then he would say, "Okay, despite my reservations we'll do it your way but let me warn you, if we don't see results by the date you promised then we're going to do it my way." Alvin was very bright about operations and his way almost always featured an emphasis on the basics. His way seldom involved much creativity, but that was not what upper management was counting on him for. They were looking for order.

In the throes of looking for another job Barry sought out Alvin. Alvin termed the training program idea "a joke" and told Barry that he could probably get a plant job for him if he were smart enough to do as he was told. Barry assured Alvin that he was and an alliance was formed. Then came the opportunity; the plant manager of the faltering St. Louis plant buckled under pressure from Alvin and quit, and Alvin asked Barry if he would like to "babysit" the plant until a new manager could be found. Barry jumped at the chance and Alvin accompanied Barry to St. Louis to show him the plant and write his script.

The plant babysitting job stretched out several months as management decided that it would be more profitable to sell the plant than to hire a new manager and attempt to turn it around. Once the plant was sold, Barry applied for the manager's job of the Louisville plant, a smaller and already profitable operation. When the executive in charge of the Louisville plant concluded the interview he instead offered Barry the sales manager's job reporting to a plant manager who was yet to be hired. Barry looked to Alvin for help but there was none. Alvin said he had nothing else to offer Barry and in any event it would be up to someone else to hire him. Of course the bridge back to accounting had already been burned and support from the executive suite had been exhausted as the rest of top management realized that Barry was clearly more interested in being in the right spot than in learning how to run a plant.

We said this story illustrated the tactical orientation to organization politics and in Barry's case that's easy to see. Barry was tactical in expressing his desire to broaden and deepen his range or organizational experience. While his words were successful in capturing top management's attention, his actions quickly revealed that he was more committed to "getting ahead" than to "learning the business." For a while Barry's tactical orientation appeared smart in that it pushed Barry ahead of the pack. But eventually it cost him the trust and confidence of those whose judgments ultimately determined how valuable Barry was considered by the organization.

To us, Alvin is the master tactician. On the surfce his organizational objectives are relatively solid. He wants excellence and high performance, and he depends on high quality performers who either will defer to his authority or who are strong enough to make it on their own. Alvin leaves people alone when they are successful and he challenges them when they are not. But he's tactical in that he is out to win every discussion and will attempt to outmuscle anyone who objects. He does not seek the other person's point of view except as it represents resistance which must be overcome. He seeks to structure each situation so that doing it his way is seen as "correct" and he is a strong enough fighter to win most of the head-to-head arguments that his combative style evokes. He intimidates people by critiquing their faults and, when they are sufficiently softened up, he offers them absolution by obtaining an agreement that, from here on out, they will do things the way he wants them done.

Alvin is successful but he lacks the trust of those who work with him. Superiors treat him as an "instrument" that must be pointed in the right direction. Subordinates recognize that loyalty to Alvin is a one-way street; five of the seven plant managers who worked under him in his prior position had been either fired or allowed to quit. They listen to him and follow his directives, but few confide their organizational weak spots or level with him about what is going wrong. Alvin has got power and people's attention, but lacks the trust-building skills he needs to create a system where the people who work for him grow and develop and where others besides himself have at least an even chance to succeed.

The Strategic Orientation

While a tactical orientation focuses on getting context in the moment, a strategic orientation focuses on using the moment to build a relationship in which others have the information and the background to make proper sense out of one's organizational actions and, most important, the inclination to use this perspective. The tactical seeks to make the best out of each situation and to gain at least a temporary advantage. The strategic seeks long-lasting strength by building a favorable context into the very fabric of a relationship.

Unfortunately, the building of such strategic relationships—ones in which people provide context for one another—requires perspectives and skills that are lacking or noticeably deficient in most people. And, these are basic relationship skills that common sense would say all responsible professionals and managers ought to possess. But they don't and that's why the tactical approach is far and away the most prevalent form of achieving context. This is unfortunate because trust depends on getting context from a relationship and not from a tactical maneuver that forces someone to agree to a proposal or to go along with a definition of reality at the expense of context for him- or herself.

We strongly believe that both the individual's and the organization's goals are best served by people taking a strategic orientation. The problem is that right now there are too many people for whom operating tactically is a kneejerk, not a deliberate response, and who, given the appropriate skills and perspectives would choose to assume a strategic orientation. Much of what follows in this book is devoted to explaining the perspectives that enable one to operate strategically. However, in reading about these perspectives it is important to bear in mind that being strategic is not synonymous with mastering a finite set of skills. Being strategic is a way of thinking about people and their pursuits, and of understanding that their needs for context are going to put them in situations where they see no alternative but to act politically. The magic in operating strategically lies not in the belief that there is a way to rise above the politics—there isn't. It comes from accepting the inevitability of the political situations that arise as people struggle to find context, and learning how to respond to these situations in ways that earn the trust and good will of those with whom one is in momentary competition.

CHAPTER 4

What People Need in Order to Achieve Context

We began this section with discussions of trust (Chapter 2) and politics (Chapter 3) because these are familiar topics in which the presence and forcefulness of the subjective element are easily visible to everyone who pays attention to what goes on at work. Both of these discussions led to a common place—context. We said that people trust those who they feel will put their efforts in the proper context and distrust those who they feel will not. We said that people are not born political animals but that their needs to be seen in the proper context drive them to behave in political ways. Now we are ready to extend our discussion of context: first, to describe its elements and exactly what images are necessary to achieve it (Chapter 4); then, to describe the political dynamics that are evoked when organizational forces deprive groups of people of one or more of these context-producing elements (Chapter 5); finally, to describe the ways managers attempt to deal with context in their efforts to create trusting relationships within the echelons that report to them (Chapter 6).

Our study of context, and each individual's need for it, allows us to be precise about defining the elements of context and what causes an individual's actions to make good organization sense. We can specify exactly what linkages must be made before others, who usually function with their own different frames of reference, can see and appreciate the real value of one's organizational contributions. People who don't understand the elements of context are subject to major difficulties in getting their talents and contributions valued. And, as a means of introducing the elements of context, we begin with an illustration of these difficulties.

Some time ago a very bright woman finishing up in our MBA program asked us to review a draft on the resumé she planned to use in her efforts to obtain a career position in the financial services industry. When we looked at her draft, something struck us as off and prompted us to ask, ''Mary Ann, where did you get the idea for this format?'' She replied, ''I saw Brad Miller's resumé on the counter when I was at the placement office last week, and when I admired it he gave me a copy. Here, look for yourself,'' and she handed us Brad's resumé.

As we compared the two, the problems with Mary Ann's resumé became clear. She was correct in thinking Brad's looked terrific; it was the model for how a strong, sharply stated, personal profile should appear. As an undergraduate, Brad had attended Stanford as a physics major and played two intercollegiate sports. His resumé was organized to emphasize his undergraduate achievements and attendance at a prestigious school, and it instantly portrayed him as someone who has what it takes to be a top-notch achiever in almost any competitive setting.

Mary Ann's mistake was in assuming that the format that portrayed the distinctive strengths and accomplishments of her classmate would do the same for her. Her life and accomplishments required more of a story. A chronological listing of her undergraduate achievements and credentials did not portray her as someone with ''fast-track'' potential. It showed that she had attended a state university where it had taken her five years to get a bachelor's degree in, of all the non-finance-relevant subjects one might choose, education. Then it showed her becoming an elementary school teacher, and taking seven years to decide to return to school to study finance and accounting. No, Brad's way of organizing his resumé did not provide Mary Ann with a very powerful self-presentation. A reader's basic impression would be well formulated before he or she got to a listing of Mary Ann's strengths and accomplishments.

As it happened, Mary Ann had turned down offers to attend first-rate universities so that she could stay at home and help her holocaust-victim parents by working full time and completing a bachelor's degree simultaneously. She subsequently obtained, on the strength of faculty recommendations, a relatively high-paying job teaching in an experimental school and doing curriculum development for the entire school district. There she authorized a commercially successful math book with a computerized instructional package to go along with it. She returned to school after her parents died when she no longer had the pressure to keep the money flowing in. Apparently she had made a good adjustment to losing her family and now had the desire to relocate and travel. Also listed but not highlighted in her resumé was the fact that she speaks six languages fluently.

We advised Mary Ann to begin her resumé with her current MBA education and a listing of her UCLA accomplishments, followed by a concise statement of her personal and career objectives and how seven years of working with math and computers helped to prepare her for a new career. We suggested that she highlight her interest in travel and fluency in languages by mentioning that she would welcome an international assignment. And we suggested that she list those languages in a separate section down below. As it turned out this was more than sufficient advice. Apparently what Mary Ann actually needed was "permission" to break from Brad's structure to develop a format better tailored to fit herself.

This incident has always stuck with us as a graphic example both of an individual's need for the proper context and the relativity of one's qualifications and merits. With only a modest effort Mary Ann was able to find a format that featured her strengths and accomplishments relative to the specific job and career she was seeking. No doubt Mary Ann was drawn to Brad's resumé because it highlighted information that portrayed him as an attractive and powerful job candidate no matter what job a company might need filled. In a highly competitive world there is a temptation to present one's relative strengths as "absolutes" which apply with equal power to all situations. But Brad is among a select few whose skills and background make him appear to be qualified for many job situations simultaneously. For most people the trick in putting together a strong resumé rests in finding a way to organize it to display their special strengths and distinctive qualities in relation to a particular setting and a particular set of job demands. That is why highlighting Mary Ann's language skills in the context of her mobility and interests in international work was so important.

Our experience counseling Mary Ann as well as others who momentarily faltered for lack of context, together with our analysis of situations in which people like Brad were immediately seen as relevant to an organization's need, have provided us with a model that explains what is necessary for an individual to establish organizational context. As we see it, three essential elements must be linked together before an individual can present him- or herself in a way that can produce context.

The first, and probably the most essential, element relates to one's organization *function*: How is the function one performs central to the productivity and well-being of the organization? The second is *role*: How does the role an individual has defined for him- or herself provide a credible and effective way of performing that function? The third is *daily activities*: How are one's daily activities viable ways of accomplishing the unique role and function one is attempting to perform? Absent any one of these connections and the individual is vulnerable—his or her contributions are subject to frames of reference that make them seem unimportant and the individual nonessential. Let's examine these elements one at a time.

Function

An individual lacks context when key others do not view the function he or she performs as central to the productivity and well-being of the organization, or when others view it as central but do not engage it in a way that allows the people performing it to be successful. Such was the situation encountered by the computer faculty recruited to the Harvard Business School during the 1960s. School administrators were excited at the prospects offered by computer technology and proud that they had made the commitment to designate computers as an area for major emphasis. However, they were also suspicious that giving them such emphasis would be license for the computer faculty to specialize in technical intricacies and miss big questions or overlook practical applications. Thus school administrators decided to treat computers as a management tool and to promote computer technology as a service to existing areas. Computer faculty members were stationed in existing groups, some in the accounting/control area and others in operations research.

Gradually, over an eight-year period, computing became an integral part of the business school's curriculum. Not only were courses taught in formal computer technology, but computing was integrated within existing courses as students were shown how to utilize the computer as a decision analysis tool. However, for those dedicated faculty members who pioneered these courses, the costs were great. While their counterparts in the other areas of the Business School were receiving recognition and being promoted on the basis of records similar to theirs, the five who shared the primary burden for introducing computer technology were denied tenure and forced to leave. And, as each new instructor replaced the last in what turned into a revolving-door process, he was told that the school recognized the problem and that the situation would soon be different. But how different could it be when the computing function was not embraced as central to the school's mission and when the computer faculty were minority members of groups with different curriculum missions?

Few would argue that the computer faculty did not serve an essential function at the Harvard Business School or that the faculty who pioneered the program did not play an important part. But the function the computer faculty served was never seen as central to the mission of the departments in which they were housed and their efforts were treated as the work of technocrats, not scholars. With such an absence of centrality, it was only a matter of time before these individuals became expendable.

Having one's function viewed as central to the productivity and well-being of one's organization is vital to having context. Being associated with a function that is not highly valued always has negative consequences even if those consequences are not immediately visible. For example, in commercial banking, activities associated with lending have been considered to be at the top of the pecking order and activities associated with operations at the bottom. In many consumer products industries, marketing and finance are at the top, and manufacturing at the bottom. Within manufacturing, production is often at the top and purchasing at the bottom. In every instance the track to promotion and upper management is much faster for individuals who work in the groups whose functions are seen as more central to the organization's mission, and therefore are perceived as having context.

Role

Anyone who has worked in an organization well appreciates how many ways there are to work at a given function. And essential to each individual's success is that he or she chooses a way of working that utilizes his or her distinctive talents. But no way of assuming a role in relation to a given function is adequate without establishing the proper context. For instance, consider the experience of two young entrepreneurs who were able to identify an unfilled function with definite commercial possibilities in a burgeoning industry, but who failed to establish credibility for the role they were taking in relation to that function.

The idea for their business originated as the two were working on a field study project at the end of their MBA course work. Their project involved market analysis and product strategy for a cable television company. Upon completion of the project, company executives were impressed to the point that they asked for more of the same and offered a contract large enough to launch the two into business. Aware that many firms needed similar assistance, the two began making calls aimed at familiarizing the industry with their service. However, they quickly found that this industry had limited experience with professional consultants and lacked a realistic picture of the fees and cost structure associated with consulting work. As a consequence the two consultants spent considerable amounts of time educating potential clients as to the areas where consultants could be of most value and with the costs associated with such services. To their surprise and disappointment their educational efforts were so successful that in three instances potential clients went out and hired competing but more established firms to perform the very studies they had promoted.

Assessing their results, these entrepreneurs learned the hard way the importance of providing others with a clear picture of the role they intended to perform and their ability to perform it. They were doing a far better job of selling the function than they were of promoting themselves as knowledgeable consultants who were as experienced as anyone in performing the work that needed to be done. For the individual desiring context, getting the organization to appreciate his or her function and its essentiality to the organization's mission is of little value if, at the same time, others do not also appreciate the individual's ability to play a key role in the delivery of that function. What's more, there are many ways to define one's role in relation to a given function, and others need to understand the specifics of the role one assumes and why that particular role definition makes organizational sense.

Daily Activities

Does sufficient context arise from having one's function viewed as central to the accomplishment of the organization's mission and one's role in the accomplishment of that mission understood and valued? This is a question we've taken to several executive education sessions in the form of a situation we encountered where this did not turn out to be enough.

This situation involved the firing of a sales manager who in less than a year had taken his division's sales from the bottom of the company to a point where sales had increased 400 percent. On the surface, his accomplishment seems to present an unassailable case of exceptional performance that should be acknowledged without challenge.

When we tell executives about this situation we do *not* mention the firing and, after reciting the facts, we ask them if they would be willing to make an unqualified judgment of whether a 400 percent increase in sales signifies an "outstanding job." As it turns out virtually no one is willing to make such a judgment without further information. Executives want to know what these results cost the overall system and what activities the sales manager actually engaged in that were central to the achieving of 400 percent results. They want to see the connection between his day-to-day efforts and his department's performance. Short of seeing this connection they can invent scores of reasons to account for the sales jump which do not involve positive efforts by the sales manager, ranging from his excessive use of advertising to an industry boom.

In the actual situation, two interconnected rationales for termination were put forth by management, each of which stressed the importance of context and the need to make others aware of how one's daily activities tie in with what one is attempting to accomplish. Management did value the sales gain but took issue with the sales manager's special need for autonomy of operation which they said resulted in an undisciplined and uneven application of efforts in sales. In addition they cited their belief that it was now time for the division to be guided by someone who could wring more profits out of the increased volume by instituting tighter controls.

Hearing this, the sales manager felt betrayed. He claimed it was his unconventional style and ability to work autonomously that had attracted management in the first place and had led them to solicit his help in bringing this sinking performer around. Now he was being criticized for utilizing the very style that they had wanted from him and was not being given a chance to show how he might operate with their new statement of goals.

From our vantage point, this sales manager lacked context. Not context that valued his function in creating a sales program that could generate sales; not context that valued the freewheeling leadership role he used in achieving sales; but context that linked his freewheeling entrepreneurial style to the activities that now needed to be accomplished in the tightening up of controls. Management could no longer see the connection between what he was doing on a daily basis and the sales that now were pouring in, and they could not envision him taking the action they would take if *they* had the responsibility to tighten up controls. Of course every manager would operate differently in the same situation, but no one asked him how he would do it.

Establishing the Elements of Context

How do people establish context? Where are the opportunities to present one's function, role, and daily activities so that others can appreciate what the individual and his or her work unit is about? How should people tell their organization story to ensure that others see the blueprint that underlies their behavior?

We have described several instances showing that people cannot count on others to place them and their work in the proper context. In fact we have found that left to their own devices others will use frameworks that are best suited to their own distinctive ways of functioning and not well tuned to appreciate another person's mode of operation. Thus people who want support for what they and their organizational unit are doing must provide others with the framework to appreciate their context. They must find ways of referencing their unit's participation so that others can understand what is intended by their behavior.

To illustrate, let's consider the situation faced by a human resource department that was struggling to change its image and to play a more powerful and essential role in the management of a large aerospace company. It's an illuminating example because few disciplines are more dependent on how others view it than human resources and few are more vulnerable to having their essence discounted and their members seen as peripheral to the organization's mission. What's more, few disciplines seek a stronger mandate and wind up with a weaker one than what human resources gets in most organizations. Everyone pays homage to the importance of people, their careers, and their training and development. Yet no set of issues, no discipline, gets shuffled to the side more quickly in the everyday conduct of business.

Back to the human resource department at our aerospace firm. What is its organizational image? How will its *function* be viewed by line management? Certainly how it is viewed will make a huge difference in the roles human-resource professionals are allowed to perform and the importance attached to their accomplishments. Will the department be seen as a support function, forming traditional labor relations, equal employment opportunity compliance, and salary administration? Or, will it be seen as a management effectiveness and development department that represents the full range of the human element in all discussions involving project planning and organizational capability? Will line management continue to value the human resource department for its traditional *after-the-fact* ability to get them out of trouble, and as a "plug-in" resource that performs specific tasks as the needs arise? Or, can they be led to value it as a department that provides an essential viewpoint—one that needs to be present *before-the-fact* when projects are proposed, when the scenarios that orient work activities are constructed, and when the problems that need to be solved are framed?

Whether it be the human resource function or any other organizational discipline, having one's efforts portrayed in the desired context entails dealing with at least three views of reality, each of which has its own subjective roots. In each situation there will be the human resource department's reality, there will be another group's reality, and there will be the reality on which members of the two groups will agree. Part of what they will agree to is determined by the realities that are already accepted as fact in their organization and part is determined by each of their respective needs to be effective and to have the stature that makes them an organizational force.

For instance, the view that human resources is a plug-in department that performs specific tasks as the needs arise may be highly compatible with the politics of the engineering department which wants to be seen as having qualified managers who are doing a solid job of resource and project management. In fact, in our aerospace company the ''plug-in'' image allows engineering managers to use Gant chart logic to reduce the human element to discrete topics that can be dealt with in the orderly chain of project events. It allows them to maintain their project dominance and to avoid sharing control. It allows them to keep all their so-called prerogatives. Likewise, the ''plug-in'' image allows other staff groups, such as marketing and finance, to experience their status as superior to those who work in human resources.

Function is the first of the elements necessary for the achievement of context. *Role* is the second. That is, the role a group defines for itself must be viewed as a credible and effective way to accomplish the function they've taken on. Everyone who works in an organization should appreciate how many ways there are to pursue a given mission. And essential to each group's effectiveness is that it finds a way of operating that capitalizes on its unique talents and resources. For instance, is the human-resource role to perform the management development function by putting on training programs for mid-level managers and supervisors and to help them enroll in courses run outside the company? Or is their role to perform the management development function through everyday project involvement in which they advise line managers on specific actions that can enhance their operating competence? In the first case, training, they need experienced trainers on their staff; in the second case, advising higher level management, they need poised consultants who tactfully can direct and coach high-ranking line managers. In either event, achieving context requires explaining their role so that what others expect is what human resources is positioned to deliver, and so that the way one defines him- or herself connects to the function that person sets out to perform.

In our model, the third and final element in the achievement of context involves developing a rationale for others to use in appreciating the group's *daily activities*. This is essential because work has now become so complex that on a daily basis almost no one produces a finished product. All that most people accomplish is "a little progress." What's more, left to one's own devices, everyone would go about making progress in a somewhat different way. Unless people tell others how their, or their group's activities are linked to the role they have designated for themselves, and the function they are endeavoring to perform, others will not understand their motivations, and the value of their efforts will be discounted.

For instance, let's say that this human resource department decides to pursue the management coaching model and that this role entails a change in orientation for some of its key staff. And to accomplish this change in orientation, let's say a training program is designed which entails human resource staff observing project planning meetings, and coming back to the human resource department to share their observations and receive instructions on how to engage in management coaching. But not everyone who observes these staff members will understand what they are up to—that their observing role is part of their training. Some will think they are intruders. These people will quickly conclude that a staff person's silent presence in another department's meeting constitutes evidence that human resources is overstaffed and is attempting to acquire more organizational power by asserting its influence in areas where it has nothing to contribute.

In an organization *all* observers—those who would like to criticize the human resource position as well as others who would like to defend it—need a framework before they can understand what is taking place. Such a framework or verbal "blueprint" can easily be provided when human resource managers remember that others cannot be expected to understand the meaning of their department's behavior merely by observing it. People have to be told. Left to their own devices, people will apply their own frames of reference, grounded in a different set of concerns, and misunderstandings about the motivations that gave rise to the observed behavior will inevitably result. Context depends on telling people how one's daily activities link both to the role one's group performs and the function they are expected to fulfill. And the statements that make up this "blueprint" can't be uttered too often.

Just as each organizational group has to develop a story that establishes its context, so does each individual. And being a part of a group that has context greatly facilitates this process. Conversely, it's extraordinarily difficult for an individual to achieve personal context when the organizational unit to which he or she belongs lacks it. How is a plausible case made for that person's value when the function performed by the organizational unit is viewed as extraneous?

Each individual needs a story that establishes his or her unique relationship to a valued function. Having the ability to tell one's story on-line, when others need to hear it, is necessary for keeping people oriented. For example, one needs the skill to say, "You do know our human resource department has changed considerably. Yes, we still provide all of the services we did when we were called industrial relations but now we perform them with a distinctly different orientation. We seek to make front-end inputs and no longer want to be seen as reactive. So while I'm still the labor-relations expert, my real goal is to get our management effectiveness viewpoint into project planning and that entails involvement with managers and planners during the periods when projects are being formulated."

When it comes to positioning one's activities, role, and functions, people often find themselves in situations where they think that their story will not be acceptable if they tell it straight. When faced with such situations many decide to present a more calculated version, one that has a greater likelihood of gaining acceptance than the "truth" as they know it. In doing so, few tell out-and-out lies—if caught the consequences and loss of credibility would be too great. However, in any organization there are countless ways to bend the truth. And the truth gets bent as much by what *isn't* said as by what people decide to say and do.

It would be ridiculous for us to moralize on this point. People seek context. How they go about achieving it depends on what they see as the stakes, and whether or not they trust those from whom they are seeking it. In any event their objective is to present themselves in an integrated fashion as an essential member of a work unit or an organization, whose function, role, and activities have high institutional value.

CHAPTER 5

Situations That Promote Organization Politics

To this point we have presented the view that politics is an inevitable by-product of each individual's struggle to gain context. In the process, however, we did not intend to leave the impression that high levels of political activity are desirable. Nothing could be further from the truth. High levels of political activity, particularly of the tactical kind, are major forms of distraction that drain energy and spirit from the workplace.

This is the chapter that sorts out the origins and costs of *excessive* levels of politics. Involvement in politics is necessary—each individual's success depends on articulating the framework that allows others to comprehend what he or she is attempting to create and its value to the institution. But when nothing an individual does produces enduring appreciation, his or her political needs take on a significantly different cast. Then people engage in politics primarily to force others to see them, their units, and/or their production in a way that will enable them to accomplish their immediate objectives. Progress made today has to be repeated tomorrow. Excessive politics is the result.

In the last chapter we delineated three elements of context and showed how each is part of the story needed to establish credibility with one's viewers. Now we must add that an individual also needs credibility with his or her own self and that these very same elements are necessary to establish it. That is, an individual needs to perform a *function* that he or she actually believes is essential to the well-being and productivity of the organization; an individual needs to perform a *role* that accomplishes an essential organization function and that utilizes his or her distinctive skills, and an individual needs to see the connection between his or her *activities* and the distinctive role and essential function he or she has actually set out to perform.

Absent any one of these elements and an individual lacks credibility—credibility with him- or herself. Lacking credibility produces feelings of insecurity and insecure feelings give rise to context-seeking activities which, depending on a viewer's orientation, are likely to be labeled political. People generally try to change or manipulate their work functions to make them more essential to the well-being or productivity of the overall organization; they attempt to redefine their roles and conduct to utilize a greater number of their distinctive skills; and they attempt to modify their activities to make them better connect with the role and function they are attempting to perform. In short, people attempt to manipulate organizational variables to produce the circumstances that provide them with a greater degree of self-context.

Acknowledging each individual's need for self-context allows us to comprehend the types of situations that deprive people of the opportunity to establish one or more elements of context and which put them on the defensive where they see no alternative but to engage in excessive amounts of the behind-the-scenes, devious, and manipulative behavior that most associate with blatant organization politics. It allows us to see how certain situations make it impossible for people to establish a stable and secure relationship with an organization so that even those who would like to get on with their work find it necessary to test the water, politicize, and actively lobby just to protect their basic credibility, let alone advocate a specific point of view. And when these situations deprive many people at a time, they set off the chain of clandestine and manipulative activities that most associate with excessively politicized organizations.

In our work we come across many excessively politicized situations. And when we talk with those managers who have the position and the power to affect them we are continually amazed. We are amazed that they are so blind to what is going on! They look around them and see the obvious symptoms—rumors, morale problems, credit stealing, firings, attempts to fix accountability by putting excessive blame on people when goals are not met—with little insight into what people need and why they are acting so political. Of course by now our readers understand that we believe that organization politics result from people lacking context, or feeling the threat of having their context taken away (notwithstanding the fact that some people are excessively greedy and compulsive in their desire for power and for them politics is a way of life). The rest of this chapter is devoted to identifying the circumstances that systematically deprive people of context and create the need for politics irrespective of the personalities involved. We have identified six such situations which will be discussed in turn.

1. Competition at the Top

In our experience the most frequent source of organization politics is excessive competition at the top. This competition may be over advocacy of specific viewpoints or values, or over people's desires for power and interests in being number one. In any event a domino effect is created whereby competitive dynamics at the top set off pressures to act politically at each echelon below. And amazing to us is the capacity of those on the top for believing that their conflict and competition is contained and not a problem for those below. So often their reactions are like those of feuding parents. They wonder what's wrong with their troubled children without realizing that their kids' problems relate to their own. Competing executives often view their own behavior as irrelevant to solving the political problems they see in the ranks below and this attitude tends to squeeze the people beneath them all the more. We've seen this attitude in the public sector, we've seen it in the private, and we wanted to include an example of each since the political forces are somewhat different.

One instance of an organization with internal political turmoil created by competition at the top occurred within an important state energy commission during the late 1970s. At the top of the commission were five governor-appointed commissioners who, as stipulated by legislation, were appointed to represent different points of view. There was an environmental appointee, whose responsibility was to advocate the conservation of natural resources; there was an industrial expansion appointee, whose responsibility was to advocate policies that provided cheap and plentiful power for industrial consumption; and there were three public appointees, each of whom was charged with representing a discipline such as economics or law along with the well-being of the general public in whatever ways they individually felt that might best be accomplished.

In concept and on paper the commission structure seemed like a wonderful idea. Energy policy would be decided in a forum in which varied and competing interests would be represented and in which no parochial point of view would dominate. However, in practice having five commissioners presented big problems for those who had the job of performing commission work.

Working for the commission was a professional staff of 400 with its own management hierarchy. While the commissioners had the job of framing issues, considering facts, and setting policy, the staff's job was to collect the data, perform the analyses, and implement the decisions taken by the commissioners as a group. The staff organization was supposed to be free to work independently of a commissioner's persuasion except that the commissioners' policy-setting rights extended to voting on key personnel appointments including those of all managers. On any given day anyone who aroused the enmity of three of the five commissioners could be voted out of a job. Of course most were protected by civil service and had a fall-back position in another agency. Nevertheless, any manager from the executive director on down could lose his or her managerial rank with barely a day's notice.

From this structure one can easily visualize the type of competition that could break out if individual commissioners failed to respect the stance another felt obligated to take. And as luck would have it, the particular mix of commissioner personalities produced just such a lack of respect and there were many times when the arguments became heated, when personalities were attacked, and when expression of different points of view became the occasion for open warfare. Adding even more pressure was the fact that this commission was often in the public limelight; it was the first to address nuclear energy issues that were to set national precedents.

Thus, whenever the competition became keen, relationships between the commisioners and the staff became especially political. Commissioners would sequester staffers, inquire how their analytic work was coming, ask what preliminary conclusions were being drawn, and then present their own interpretations with innuendos that anyone seeing the results differently ought to have his or her head examined. Then they implied that just such an examination might take place during a closed-door hearing of the five commissioners.

From the staff perspective, the situation was an organizational nightmare. As one manager put it, "It's like having five different bosses, each with his own independent viewpoint, with the added twist that none of the commissioners takes any responsibility for the fact that we have to deal with an associate's points of view." Predictably, staff members became quite cautious and began spending a high percentage of their work time trying to figure out how to keep each of the commissioners happy, and thinking about how to defend themselves against those from within their own ranks who had aligned themselves with a particular commissioner. The result was a staff that often took refuge in verbose, highly technical language and bland reports. Staff relations with the commissioners degenerated into a game of pretending that each commissioner's interests came first. In effect the staff attempted to play off one commissioner's biases against another's.

We recognize that an organizational setting in which each manager has five bosses who don't get along represents an extreme situation. Nevertheless it's a situation that illustrates the problems associated with developing self-context when one lacks a stable frame of reference at the top. People need context, and when it's not forthcoming from the organization, they attempt to get it by erecting a framework of their own. But, because they cannot be explicit about the role they are pursuing and the stance they are taking, they act politically. They develop alliances to protect them while they covertly follow a substitute direction which, in their own minds, is superior to, or at least as good as, the directions given to them by the top. Thus the commissioners' inability to articulate a coherent point of view rendered the organization

vulnerable to covert views that, in many instances, were excessively self-indulgent and at odds with a direction that even the
commissioners had agreed to among themselves. Apparently
there is a level of participation in which politics take on a runaway
dimension where people can no longer discriminate between
what's necessary in order to cope and political behavior as a way
of life.

In the private sector politics rarely have their origins in situations like the one described above. If there is one thing that top
managers in the private sector know, it's how to isolate and center
responsibility and to hold operating levels accountable. Nevertheless, when competition breaks out at the top, it produces political
binds that people in the levels below find every bit as intense and
unnerving. For instance, we are intimately familiar with a con-
glomerate that put its entire operating management through a
painful exercise when two top-level executives started fighting.
The circumstances were straightforward and easily understandable—each of these men needed different contexts in order to feel
secure and powerful.

> The conglomerate was a group of sixteen companies with a
> strong-willed founder/chairman of the board who was past re-
> tirement age. There were two senior managers, one in charge
> of operations and the other in charge of finance; one of them
> would become the chairman's successor. The operations man
> held the title of corporation president and had been raised in
> the parent industry, which for the sake of anonymity we'll call
> the transportation business. He was using that industry's ac-
> counting framework as the basis for monitoring and overseeing
> each of the acquired businesses. The finance man held the title
> of executive vice-president. He was relatively new to the cor-
> poration, had never worked in the transportation business,
> and had experience in several industries. He contended that
> the transportation model was wrong for the conglomerate as a
> whole and that each of the acquired businesses had distinctive
> components and facets to which the transportation experience
> was insensitive and which his department was well equipped
> to handle if only operations would accept a new system.
>
> Behind this dispute was the ambivalence of the chairman of
> the board about letting go. As long as his top level executives
> fought, his presence was essential. His support of each and re-

fusal to declare his own deciding point of view kept the competition going. Each executive had to dig in or be seen as capitulating. There was nowhere to retreat. In an attempt to settle this conflict the finance man created an organizational exercise. Under the guise of ''business systems planning,'' a task force was created to conduct an in-depth study of each of the company's sixteen businesses and to recommend whether or not a new set of categories should be used in monitoring the activities, results, and profits of each of the groups. To insure that its findings would be seen as valid, only people with the most impeccable credentials were appointed to the task force.

Once the finance man created the task force the president might as well have started packing. There was no way a group of managers with different businesses would agree with the transportation model. They didn't, and when the study was concluded the president was allowed to resign. So were several senior executives who had been schooled in the transportation business and who had relocated in other divisions. The finance man immediately succeeded the president, but the recommendations for a new system were only partially implemented. Today it's a new situation. There's another fight, with the new president holding the line on the modified system he instituted, and a new protagonist arguing for a different model. The Chairman is still holding on, unconsciously fueling the flames. And the pressures continue to filter down. Today's pressure is for short-term immediate profits with deep cutbacks in personnel, moratoriums and ceilings on salary increases, and curtailment of internal functions that have long-term payback periods such as R&D.

In our experience top-level shootouts are never contained. We've never seen them take place without affecting a large part of an organization. For instance, in the aforementiond example there are senior managers in each of the sixteen companies who are so afraid of becoming a fatality in the next purge that they shun lining up with any identifiable viewpoint that might later place them in conflict with a new perspective that emerges at corporate headquarters. Most are biting their tongues and running their businesses as if monthly statements are the only navigational tools needed to chart a course or to measure their division's progress.

Common to both of these illustrations is instability at the top. Organization politics are a common response when people find themselves in situations where disagreements at the top deprive them of organizational context—of a stable framework against which they can reference their organization actions and link them to the good of the whole. In its absence people devise statements of function for themselves which are born in self-interests, covertly pursued, and which become sources of daily political tension. Thus people engage in the machinations that they believe will provide the self-context needed to be an organizational and personal success. The lack of a stable point of view, however, need not result from multiple bosses using different perspectives. It can just as easily result from the erratic behavior of a single boss.

2. The Erratic Boss

Some months ago a colleague asked us to counsel a friend of his who was spending sleepless nights worrying about his new job. We agreed and made a date to see him. When the friend came over he gave us all the cues that he expected a long conversation and was surprised when the conversation concluded twenty-five minutes later.

> The friend came in, took out his cigarettes and lighter and arranged them along with his keys on the table. He accepted our offer of coffee, discovered he had two cigarettes lit at once, looked extremely anxious, thanked us for seeing him, and got right into relating his predicament. He was a professional photographer who had been working for three months as a photographic editor of a female-oriented equivalent of *Playboy* magazine. He told us that he was heterosexual, had never photographed men before, didn't know women's tastes in beefcake, and had a too-short boss who seemed to enjoy pushing him, at six feet two, around. We asked how others got along with the boss? When he said, "They think the boss is crazy and complain he is always changing his mind about what he wants," we said, "Quit."

We told "the friend" to quit because it was clear that he was in a situation in which self-context could never be attained. He had an essential function he did not feel competent to perform, lacked the skill to perform his role distinctively, and did not have an orientation that would allow him to be confident that his activities would eventually accumulate to accomplish a distinct role and essential function. What's more, he had a boss who would not lend him a stable frame of reference to use until he could develop his own. What could be worse than not being confident of the judgments one has to make, having a boss whose framework seems more dependent on internal emotional processes than on external facts, and lacking the experience needed to take a stand when one thinks him- or herself correct?! It puts an individual in a situation where his or her bearings and success totally depend on the whims of an inconsistent evaluator. This forces a person to cultivate that relationship on far less than honest grounds.

The pervasiveness of problems with erratic bosses was demonstrated to us through a peculiar set of circumstances. We had consented to an interview by a *Los Angeles Times* reporter who was developing an article on "crazy bosses" and the effect their erratic behavior had on the people who worked for them. Once we figured out what she was up to we advised her to change the title from "Crazy Bosses" to "Crazy-Making Bosses." We reasoned that bosses with deep emotional problems are relatively easy to spot and, once recognized, relatively easy to discount. On the other hand, those we label "crazy-making" have a style that makes it very difficult for people to achieve context and their destructive impact is often difficult to see. We reasoned that individuals are emotionally vulnerable when they depend on a boss who either lacks the ability to affirm their context or is competitive with them and has no interest in doing so. We described how a boss with a need for a context that is incompatible with a subordinate's could drive that person nuts while not posing a particular problem for others whose needs for context are more compatible.

Fortunately for the reporter, she decided to stick with the Crazy Boss title and her article was a big success. Not only did it appear on the front page of the *Times* but it was syndicated in at least twenty other major publications. Despite our errant advice, our views were given prominent attention with the result that we were deluged with calls, letters, and even a telegram from individuals whose lives the article had touched. We had grossly underestimated the number of people who are caught in destructive relationships with their bosses and who think that they, themselves, are the cause of their problems. For them, an article that labeled their boss "crazy" was a revelation providing doubts that the strife they had been experiencing was of their own making.

We heard many stories—stories of the ways people found to compensate for the problems created by having a boss who gives no support to their needs to be valued and seen as relevant to the organizational setting in which they were expected to perform. It was in relation to these conversations that we were exposed to accounts of flagrantly devious, clandestine, and malicious political behavior initiated not by the "crazy" bosses but by otherwise rational and positively inclined subordinates who happened to have the misfortune to land in a position that deprived them of context and a chance for success. While many told stories of trying to escape, most had what they saw as darn good reasons for staying where they were and working behind the scenes for their bosses' demise. They also were working diligently to publicize the value of what they produced in an effort to compensate for their apparent lack of context.

We'll spare the specifics because they are not necessary to make our point. Any set of circumstances, such as that described in our metaphor of the "erratic boss," which makes it difficult or impossible to get context, creates the conditions for political conniving among otherwise wonderful people of the caliber of you and us. People who cannot find a niche within the established structure are forced to create their own, and the means they use often serve to politicize the environment in which they and their cohorts work.

3. Too Much Hierarchy

Consistently we have found that organizations with excessive levels of hierarcy are hotbeds of political activity. And when we stopped to think about this the reason was quickly apparent. Too much hierarchy crowds people so that performing an essential function involves variables over which the individual lacks sufficient control; so that a role that capitalizes on the distinctive strengths of an individual usually involves responsibilities and duties that are assigned to someone else; and so that there are too many constraints to performing the activities that make sense in the pursuit of an essential function and distinctive role to which the individual is attached. In short, excessive hierarchy makes it impossible for people to find self-context because there is not a whole job for them to perform.

We have found that most organizations contain at least one extra level of hierarchy. Its existence serves to assure management that all important functions will be performed. And in our experience one extra level does little harm when there's enough real work to keep people busy. Then people at various levels extend above and below themselves to make sure a responsibility is covered, or a project accomplished, without taking anything essential away from others. However, problems resulting in excessive politics arise when there is more than one extra level of hierarchy, for then people's incursions to levels above or below threaten the integrity of the jobs of those whose territory is being entered.

In organizations, people get context from performing an entire job. Whether one's job is that of division manager, section head, or first-level supervisor, as long as the boundaries are clearly delineated and understood, people have the opportunity to succeed. But when the boundaries are not clear and people lack the authority to keep others from overlapping their responsibilities and functions, such as the situations that accompany too much hierarchy, people become fearful. Then they need assurances that cooperation with the other person, and solving the overlap in responsibilities by making it a team effort, will be recognized and valued by the organization. If such assurances are not adequate or forthcoming, people will engage in political jockeying. They attempt to manipulate organization roles and responsibilities so that they can once again perform an entire function. Usually this means stealing parts of someone else's job, not necessarily in an effort to attain more power and prestige, but in an effort to establish the minimal conditions for self-context and thus create the circumstances that are necessary to succeed.

Such personal maneuvering has often gone on at the Pentagon, an organization in which almost everyone has overlapping responsibilities and one that periodically accumulates hierarchy piled on top of hierarchy. At regular intervals reformers are sent in to streamline things, but, typically, a new organization is barely in place before some manager becomes concerned that this or that responsibility is not being covered, or is not receiving sufficient priority, and decides to invent a supplemental group that overlaps an existing unit. Once established, the original unit senses the redundancy, becomes blatantly territorial, and wide-ranging political machinations break out. And one doesn't have to go to the Pentagon to see such dynamics. They can appear in any organization and take place whenever a manager attempts to cope with distrust by inventing a supplemental or slave organization. We've seen a manufacturing department invent its own engineering group that eventually competed with the company's engineering department; we've seen a sales group invent its own marketing unit that eventually caused conflicts both with division and corporate marketing; and we've seen executives hire consultants whose opinions were more like theirs and whose presence supplanted the authority of line managers and other key staff who might disagree with them.

In recent years there have been many expert-led experiments in which hierarchies of people are brought together to examine an entire system with the intent of reevaluating jobs and redesigning them to feature more efficiency and greater effectiveness. While these analyses are almost always conducted as open-ended experiments, with the results neither fixed in advance nor prejudged, all the experiences of which we know have pointed in the same direction. Hierarchies are streamlined to feature fewer jobs with bigger functions. This differs significantly from the conclusions reached when only the upper echelons are involved, for they usually create more jobs with finer breakdowns in function.

While most experiments in job redesign have been directed towards manufacturing operations and what takes place on the shop floor, our own work has involved managers and professionals such as engineers and accountants. Our results are consistent. When viewing the entire system, people always see the problems and inefficiencies that result when their jobs overlap others and they recommend changes that provide larger jobs and less controlled supervision. People instinctively trust and have confidence in the actions of those who have achieved context, and given the opportunity they will attempt to incorporate the conditions that produce context. What's more, engaging in such analyses seems to enlighten people about what others need in the way of context while, at the same time, engendering support for like needs of their own.

4. Insufficient Respect for the Individual

Too many managers talk as if they have a *"magic door"* behind which a line of competent performers stand waiting to take the place of the incompetent person they have just observed. It's as if all one has to do to get rid of one's problems is to open the door and let in the next person in line. We can't begin to tell you how many variations we've heard on this one. Perhaps it's merely a wish that managers utter out loud, perhaps it's merely a cry of frustration, but whatever it is, it's disorienting. The notion that problems can be solved easily by replacing people prevents managers from seeing that others need self-context in order to perform effectively.

Whenever someone important begins to think in "magic door" terms, politics run rampant. And in our experience, whether or not people actually are replaced makes little difference. Making a mistake, failing to produce what one sets out to produce, performing less ably than someone else expects, and not contributing in the proper form become too important. In response people spend long hours figuring out what their bosses expect and attempt to produce it in the proper form while giving only secondary consideration to the appropriateness of what they are doing. They deny their errors and attempt to hide whatever might frustrate someone else's expectations. Power politics become the order of the day as wordsmithing, logrolling, and lobbying become intense

In the situation we're describing, evaluation is severe and justice occurs in the minds of the evaluators, not in the minds of the judged. An inadequate system of forgiveness exists. In such situations, criticisms become more than just statements of how an individual performed in a given role; they become attacks on an individual's stature. People experience themselves being viewed as objects, as entities that are supposed to accomplish this or that—and not as complete human beings with strengths, needs, and imperfections, human beings who are sometimes strong and sometimes vulnerable and who on any given day are capable of "blowing one." Magic-door thinking strips people of their complexity, deprives them of self-context, and leaves them with little choice but to act political.

Happily there are some organizations where people are treated respectfully and with the proper amount of support and security to insure that they have context and perform at their best. In fact we know of a company, in which one of us spent seven years working as a management consultant, that gets high grades in the dimension of showing respect for people and their needs for context. This is a large consumer products company that has long been included on lists of best managed companies. We liked the respectful way they treated people long before we started thinking about the causes of organizational politics.

At Acme, our fictitious name for the company, people are treated respectfully at every stage of their careers. The emphasis is on succeeding—not in being punished for one's mistakes. No one ever criticizes others in public although they often make tough-minded statements about what a program needs in order to operate more effectively. At Acme, bosses are held responsible for their subordinates' performance and are not given the latitude to blame their inability to produce on the individuals who work for them. But even behind closed doors the poor performers are treated with dignity. Instead of being disgraced, they are given less demanding assignments.

Organizational structure changes frequently at Acme and people are transferred from one function and one department to another without a clear understanding of which job has the higher status. The important thing is to achieve context by becoming a member of a winning team. At Acme the emphasis is always on market competition, rather than competition within the ranks, and when a product wins in the marketplace everybody connected with that product advances.

It's seldom that someone at Acme gets both a promotion and a significant salary increase at the same time. Because of this, people who outlive their usefulness in one role can readily be transferred laterally without a pay change until they find a niche where they can perform effectively. There are "fast-trackers" at Acme and people cheer for them because they are seen as having the ability to pull a project along with everyone on the successful team getting one benefit or another. This produces an excessive reliance on one's team role as the basis for self-context and some people who leave Acme have difficulties putting their needs for context back on more individualistic terms. They take at face value what people in their new organization have promised and don't adequately check to see that what was promised will actually be delivered the way it always is at Acme.

We think that one of the best parts of the Acme spirit is that people seldom gossip disrespectfully about one another. Acme is relatively free of the types of put-downs and contemptuous statements we hear so often in the corridors, closed offices, and cafeterias of other companies. People attempt even-handed assessments of others even when voicing an out-and-out complaint. They seek to put shortcomings in the context of people's strengths; they attempt to cite what the supporters feel alongside of what the critics say. They attempt to keep their critical comments specific to a particular incident, saying something like, "I don't like the way John did that." They refrain from making criticisms that generalize to all situations or downplay the importance and general ability of the person who is the target of their critique. And when they can't respect the person, they attempt to show respect for that person's job or title.

Perhaps the core of the Acme system is that Acme management never forgets that everyone has a technical job to perform. For all its emphasis on people, Acme's management reserves its biggest rewards for technical contributors, considering marketing and managerial success to be technologies that parallel the scientific and manufacturing disciplines without implying a pecking order. At the upper levels of management, it makes no difference whether one's expertise is in manufacturing, R&D, marketing, or engineering. Candidates from each discipline are considered on the basis of their general business acumen; there are no fixed preferences for one discipline over another. Thus, throughout the company there is the belief that technical skills are necessary in order to be ranked high enough to be considered for management, that general management skills are necessary for promotion, and that anyone in the company, no matter what his or her discipline, can become the company's president.

5. Too Much Job Security

We've consistently seen politics run rampant in situations in which people with context have insufficient incentive to worry about the context needs of those who don't. This often happens in organizations where people are sure that they won't be fired, such as in some echelons of government, where people are protected by civil service or patronage, in some areas of academia, where professors are protected by tenure, in the post office, where no one ever seems to rock the boat, and in pockets within the private sector, often in profitable operations that have yet to experience market adversity.

Without the incentive to consider actively how the current situation hampers others, those who have self-context or who have "secure" jobs resist appeals for change and possible improvement. They act to hold off customers who would like a change in product or service and they act to hold off appeals by people within their organization who lack context and would like to play a more significant role in the organization's accomplishments. And regardless of which side one is on, the situation quickly turns political.

Needing context, needing to renegotiate the organization's roles and functions, and encountering those who appear not to even allow the renegotiating conversation to be raised sends one off thinking about all the circuitous and indirect routes that might provoke a change. People resort to asking themselves "Who do I know at City Hall and how can I position my appeal to get him or her to straighten out this situation?" Conversely people who experience extraordinary and indirect pressures quickly perceive themselves to be in a political role and actively begin to respond appropriately. Now they can further justify their steadfast resistance on the grounds that their integrity depends on holding off those who seek to use "illegitimate" means to get them to change.

We see no need to illustrate this situation. It is familiar to everyone who has ever shaped an appeal to someone else who is not listening with an open mind. When the appeal is important, when one's self-context depends on it, usually the means for getting that person's ear materializes. Sufficient motivation is all that is necessary to trigger a political action.

6. Fixation with the Bottom Line

We want to mention one other situation that predictably triggers a political response. We mention it briefly because so much has already been written about it and we don't want to be redundant. It's the lesson from Japan, the lesson of "Big Auto" and "Big Steel," the lesson of any corporation whose ownership has switched from shareholders taking a long-term perspective to short-term speculators who need an extra dime of quarterly profit in order to keep the price of the company's stock moving up.

When you stop and think about it, it's easy to see why an emphasis on short-term tangible results leads directly to organization politics. How many people do you know who would, of their own volition, choose to define the value of their organizational existence solely on the basis of a short-term tangible indicator? It's a very narrow and, ultimately, self-alienating way to define one's context and value to the organization—even when one succeeds in producing the bottom-line numbers that signal success. And, for the organization, such tactics produce individual success at the price of integration, no matter how clever organization designers are at constructing the bottom-line criteria. Whenever management substitutes bottom-line criteria for the conversations necessary to produce results, in order to squeeze out the slack, people get inventive and devious in pursuing the actions that will give them the context they need to lead personally satisfying and organizationally valued lives at work.

The Most Political Organization We've Ever Seen

We've presented these six situations that frustrate people's needs for self-context as if they are discrete conditions that exist in a pure form. In practice these conditions overlap, and it's seldom that you will find one condition without also encountering the presence of one or more others. In fact we can think of a company in which pieces of each condition exist, and it has to be the most political and least healthy situation we've come across yet. Ironically, this unhealthy company is in the health insurance business. Examining it illustrates how the conditions we've mentioned combine to produce behaviors that are stereotypically political.

For the sake of anonymity we refer to this company as the First Aid Medical Insurance Company. It's a profitable company, not because it operates efficiently, but because its not-for-profit status allows it to pass all operating costs along to its consumers, much as a public utility can, in the form of increased premiums. What's more, feedback time from the marketplace is slow so that the impact of uneconomical decisions today often will not be felt internally for two or more years. It's a company that has benefited greatly from being in the right place at the right time, and its growth has been substantial. And it's a company that is being ruled with an iron hand by a single executive whose political instincts and skills in dealing with diverse and competitive viewpoints have created an aura of invincibility. He knows how to balance the complex interests of such diverse parties as health providers, hospitals, companies that buy insurance plans, claimants, third-party insurers, and a host of legislative and governmental regulators. But internally the organization is a mess.

To begin with, nothing significant happens inside this company without the big boss being involved. He participates in every supervisory and managerial promotion, every change in the organization chart, every modification of the physical facility, and he almost single-handedly makes all the high-level decisions himself. Reporting to him are five vice-presidents and several administrative types. None of these people is especially bright, all are very afraid of him, and each can tell a story of how the big boss hit the ceiling when "so and so" was dumb enough to say "whatever" in a meeting. Each has been that "so and so" and has undergone more than one public scolding.

One would think that the five vice-presidents would band together against the tyranny and harrassment of this erratic boss, but this has not been the case. We're not sure whether it's instinctive genius or sadism that causes the boss periodically to reorganize the company so that masses of people, sometimes several hundred at a time, find themselves reporting to a different vice-president. Three of these vice-presidents are older, without particular ambition, and take these shifts with a grain of salt. The other two are young enough to think about being the boss's replacement when he retires or perhaps accepts a government appointment, which, because he's wealthy and 64 years old, could happen at any time. And when the music in this game of musical chairs stops, they want to be standing in front of a large organization.

Talk about hierarchy, we've never seen so much extra hier-

archy as that which exists at First Aid. Very few people seem to
have entire jobs, and everyone seems to have enormous
amounts of free time, much of which is spent in the company's
luxurious dining area conducting private campaigns and col-
lecting the information that will enable them to do a bigger
job. People are constantly trying to steal responsibility from
those above, below, or alongside of themselves; those who
aren't successful in stealing enough responsibility to perform
an entire job seem to sublimate by gossiping about who has
been able to and who is on top of things today.

It's very hard to find context in this company. Because of
the extraordinary power of the big boss, everyone positions
him- or herself in relation to the boss's position. But his position is impossible to predict since most of his viewpoints are
dictated at least partially by his constituencies outside the
company, about which few people know the details. The best
people seem able to do is to avoid winding up on the wrong
side of an issue. And the need to avoid being wrong has
reached overwhelming proportions. It's gotten to the point
where one can't get anyone to agree to anything of substance
prior to running a trial balloon past the executive suite. In fact
we can't remember the last time we heard anyone give an une-
quivocal "yes"; the most affirmative response we hear is "I
wouldn't disagree with that." And instead of saying "no,"
people say "I don't think *Mr. Big* would like that."

Perhaps the most telling symptom of this extraordinarily
political environment is the amount of time people spend
planning what they are going to say when they get in the room
with the higher-level person they want to influence. At First
Aid people spend enormous amounts of time rehearsing and
attempting to anticipate the reaction they might receive. And
while this holds for every level of the hierarchy, it's particularly
true for conversations with *Mr. Big*. There are any number of
stories about a person who inadvertently said the "wrong"
thing or showed a lack of respect in a meeting with *Mr. Big* and
how *Mr. Big* didn't even bother to respond, wouldn't dirty his
hands, and the next morning the offender's desk was empty.
Whether or not these stories are true makes little difference;
they reflect what people think is taking place at First Aid.

"Don't surprise your boss" is a sacred slogan at First Aid.

One manager described his relationship with his boss this way:

> On the way in they explained to me that he was someone who had long ago retired on the job. But I got taken in by his opening words. He told me he was going to take an active interest in my work, so I kept him informed on a daily basis. Then I began to get the message, although I can't even tell you the form in which it came. But eventually I got it: "Keep me clean, don't let me be surprised, make enough contact to give others the impression that we're communicating and in return I'll front for you and give you good ratings." So now we meet three half-hour sessions a month and during that time he keeps me well informed on his golf game.

Job security is a curious commodity at First Aid. Occasionally there is a big scandal, such as the time someone inadvertently made an incorrect entry on the company's large computer and turned up records of an upper-level manager's private business. However, after that manager was fired, he went into business for himself and today is an outside vendor earning more money selling services to First Aid than he earned when he was working full time for the company. But short of scandals First Aid uses a no-layoff policy. And since the demands for most people's performance are modest, many people slip into a low level of self-expectation and begin to wonder how they could survive if they ever left. There's a family atmosphere, and most managers' styles can be described as benevolently paternalistic. People are paid comparable wages whether or not they perform well. Of course, nonperformers spend much of their time conducting campaigns to tell others about how hard and intelligently they are working.

There's not much else to say about First Aid. It's a culture where many people have been knocked around, demoted, and then allowed to continue. It's a culture where personal relationships are very central to one's job success, where numerous people have risen quickly based on the strength of a relationship with a higher-up. And it's a culture where the people who are negatively affected by a managerial decision often receive their bad news in a public meeting where they can be embarrassed. Because of this, the grapevine has grown to new heights of importance. People work hard to get the information that helps them avoid being surprised, and every day there is a new scramble to achieve some semblance of self-context.

Conclusion

We find it relatively easy to diagnose a company's ills when we hear stories of large numbers of people acting very politically. We know that something in the company's structure or environment is preventing people from getting context and that they are reduced to coping moment by moment. Fixing the situation entails identifying what is systematically depriving people of context and then engineering a solution. Seldom does the actual fixing involve negotiating between personalities, although interpersonal work is often necessary to repair relationships that were damaged while the individuals were engaged in survival functioning. On the other hand we find that many people take politically explosive situations very personally, impute the most negative motives to those who "abused" them during the fray, and hold deep resentments and feelings of betrayal. With these people we call attention to the structural elements that made it impossible for the people they resent to operate differently. After all, we counsel, their needs for self-context were severely frustrated. With those who can't get past their resentments and whose feelings of distrust linger long after the situation is repaired, we describe how these resentments have become a self-fulfilling prophesy and counsel them to leave. At work, or at home, it is not possible to have a healthy relationship when one of the participants operates with distrust and smoldering resentments. In such situations no-fault divorce appears to be the treatment of preference.

CHAPTER 6

How Management Creates Trust

Two key ideas were advanced in Chapter 5. First, organizations frequently operate in ways that make it difficult or impossible for people to get context. Second, when people lack context they have little choice but to act politically, and this comes at the cost of trusting relationships. The strong image, advanced in Chapter 5, of organizations thwarting the individuals's ability to achieve context, raises some fundamental issues regarding the importance management attaches to trust, the means management has at its disposal for helping people put others in context, and the kind of managerial support people can count on receiving in their efforts to achieve context and develop trusting relationships.

From our perspective, there are two approaches to forming trusting relationships within organizations. Both of them deserve the support of management, but only the first receives it. Both of these approaches depend on people having the inclination and the skills to view one another in the proper context. And both depend on people seeing that this is what the other intends to do. Conversely, distrust is produced when one person lacks the inclination, lacks the skills, or has the inclination and the skills but is not able to communicate that he or she is implementing them.

The first approach is the one we call *shared fate* and is the trust-building method that management has used for years. It is the approach that most people relate to team play on the athletic field. Trust is created as a result of people seeing themselves united in a common pursuit and seeing that their associates have the desire and know-how to pursue that goal in a mutually compatible way. In theory, each person is asked to subordinate his or her personal goals to those of the team and does so because the situation is structured so that everyone shares in the team results. The fact that each person is interested in a similar set of outcomes establishes a situation where people have similar needs for context, and this leads them to interpret events and perceive reality in mutually compatible ways. In such instances one individual's self-interested pursuits are expected to bear fruit for another, and trust between two people accrues to the extent that neither person sees the pursuits of the other coming at the expense of what else he or she holds as high priority.

We call the second approach *respect for individual differences*. Most people associate this approach with what exists between work associates who are friends but whose needs do not always overlap. Again, each individual's need for context is central. However, unlike shared fate, this approach does not assume that people are always working for the same goals or that their needs for context are not in competition. It does assume that people have the capacity to learn what lies behind what the other advocates, to respect the other person's different needs and inclinations, and to demonstrate what the other will perceive to be fair play in representing their different views of reality.

Few managers understand the intricacies involved in the *individual differences* approach nor do they possess the technology and the patience for putting it into action. Moreover, comprehending it also relies on understanding that each individual has unique needs for context, and on appreciating the political circumstances each individual encounters when dealing with the reality that someone else asserts. These are perspectives that most managers lack, and even those who have them seem to lack the interpersonal know-how to put them into action. In contrast, many strategies for promoting trust and developing trusting relationships have been developed using the shared fate approach, and are being utilized today in the spirit of promoting organization effectiveness.

Shared Fate

In almost every job, managers are instructed in how shared fate can be used to produce high levels of teamwork and cooperation. The lore on organizations is replete with stories describing instances where getting a business off the ground or averting a major crisis was of such superordinate importance that everyone could depend on each of their cohorts to the hilt. Such stories describe how everyone devoted total energy to the organization cause and emphasize how a shared sense of destiny instilled in each person a readiness to place maximum value on what each of the others contributed and to credit each of them as an essential component in producing valuable results.

It was during the aftermath of World War II that American management began an active search for techniques and devices to institutionalize what we're calling the shared fate approach. This was the time when dealing with world markets became so complex, when product lines became so diverse, and formal lines of communication became sufficiently overextended, that managers searched for ways to avoid leaving trusting relationships to chance. Techniques were sought to structure work relationships so that people who were supposed to cooperate experienced a shared fate. For instance, responding to their companies' enormous growth in product lines and involvement in diverse markets (defense, industrial, consumer) top managers at firms like General Electric and DuPont attempted to break their companies down into more manageable units. They did this by divisionalizing and by pioneering the use of profit centers so that managers who work together could better trace their unit's effectiveness and see how their combined effort affected overall company performance. What's more, discrete units gave executives the tools they needed to hold groups of managers accountable. Corporate and divisional performance were broken down into measurable units and executives were able to assert control.

Numerous refinements were added to divisionalization, each aimed at capitalizing on the benefits of putting people in situations where they could see their common goals and experience a shared fate. The idea was to identify a group goal and to structure the incentive system so that the goal's place in what motivates an individual was sufficiently high to transcend that person's self-centered interests and to override his or her inclination to compete with other members of the so-called "team." Most of these approaches attempted to relate financial results to team performance. Using indices such as net operating profit (NOP), return on investment (ROI), and market share over the previous year (MSOPY), management attempted to instill in its personnel a feeling of shared fate and a motivation towards a common goal.

Following the establishment of shared financial targets was a second wave of approaches aimed at personalizing one's feeling of shared fate and team commitment. These approaches attempted to link specific behavioral acts to key financial and operating results. The idea was to draw a stronger connection between everyday activities and the bottom line. Such approaches included "management by objectives" and "business planning," each of which requires people to declare their individual objectives before the fact and to identify specific plans to make a positive impact on sales, production, and profitability. These approaches have produced an emphasis on statistics as people attempt to measure their efforts by such means as billable hours worked, sales calls per day, and even recruiting interviews per acceptance. Today all of these approaches have been augmented with elaborate bonus and incentive systems aimed at, among other things, supporting the feeling that group or team-level performance is essential to the individual's success.

Shared fate works; there is no disputing this. However there are problems. The biggest problem lies in situations where management inappropriately attempts to use it on people who do not see their goals overlapping. More than ever before people are in touch with their self-interests and are likely to recognize when they are being asked to pursue an externally imposed goal that lacks personal meaning. What's more, people are better than ever at faking it, at saying the "right" thing and presenting the illusion that they have bought into a set of team objectives while they continue to pursue their own course. The smart people do not lose track of their needs for context even when they speak the words that need to be spoken in order to give the impression that they are loyal to the shared fate images that their superiors have advanced. After all, no one wants to be caught acting individualistically in a situation that calls for team play.

Another problem with the shared fate approach lies with its dependence on periodic crisis. The artificial goals that management creates, and the devices they use for measuring progress against these goals, produce periodic crises that give management the opportunity to focus team energy and call for heroic efforts to avert the imagined calamity. The problem is that this approach becomes addictive as crises of increasing scale become the only available means for creating teamwork. Such pressure tactics are probably not a good long-term approach to use with a work force that is becoming increasingly independent. More than ever before, today's work force is mobile, conscious, self-directed, and skeptical about the possibility of exploitation. Job heroics and deferred living no longer result in more commitment; they result in the circulation of resumés. Artificial production of crises, in the service of creating teamwork, will buy only a limited amount of allegiance. People quickly tire of the drills and move on.

Sometimes a shared fate appeal is used in situations where people are primarily interested in being recognized as special. In many professions, notably advertising, sales, consulting, upper management, and public office, people recognize that their success depends on personal recognition and that they need to be in situations where their uniqueness and individuality are recognized. In such instances, a shared fate appeal for teamwork produces conflict and cynicism. People see themselves as having little to gain by identifying with what's been proposed as a team outcome, certainly much less than the person who made the proposal, and thus resist.

The above is not to suggest that the shared fate approach is completely bankrupt. Rather, it has been overworked and abused to the point where its effectiveness has been diminished. The original spirit of shared fate has been progressively violated. It's one thing for management to emphasize bona fide external challenges and crises as a means of galvanizing internal solidarity. It's another to use ''bottom-line'' measures to manufacture crisis after crisis as a means of maintaining control. Today's management is often guilty of indiscriminately using bottom line results as a whip for generating organizational energy to such a degree that ''the game'' has become obvious to all but the most naive. There are only so many times one can hear the cry of ''wolf'' before the desired response is extinguished.

Respect for Individual Differences

Almost everyone in a large organization has one or two trusting relationships that are not based on shared fate but, in fact, are with people whose personal pursuits and organizational goals are substantially different from their own. These are relationships in which people's trust for one another is not based on sameness and similarity, although they may have a lot in common both personally and situationally. These are relationships where trust is based on personal familiarity to the extent that, when viewing the person's organizational behavior, each has a good idea of the special talents and inclinations that spark the other person's commitments—where the other person is coming from, and where that person is heading. Moreover, these are relationships in which each understands that the other is inclined to give a supportive interpretation and will ask questions when some action fails to compute with their expectations. In short, these are relationships in which the participants are committed to putting one another in the proper context.

Usually those who participate in such relationships are quite aware of their differences but try to minimize their negative impact and even seem to derive enjoyment from viewing the same events differently. They can do this because their relationship is characterized by a bond of loyalty and trust that both believe will last forever, and it often does. While these relationships have a social dimension that includes spontaneous office drop-ins and lunching together, they often are confined to business hours and center on issues generated in the course of one's work.

Most often, this type of trusting relationship is acquired before the differences between participants matter materially in the daily conduct of business affairs. Frequently it is the result of serendipitous circumstances in which private thoughts are shared and in which some essential aspect of the participants' values and character is exposed. Business travel, enduring some organizational crisis together, being taken under someone's wing when new to the company, being from the same home town, or roommates at a training program, are among the serendipitous circumstances people cite when explaining how they and the person they trust built their bond.

People get a great deal out of such trusting relationships. They use them as sounding boards, for blowing off steam, for exchanging grapevine intelligence, for good-natured gossiping, and, most importantly, for advice when the going gets rough. They can share weaknesses, problems, and even vent their guilts. They can use them to discuss their triumphs openly and to brag without fearing jealousy or overly competitive reactions. They can do this because they know that the other person understands where they are coming from and can appreciate the unique meaning that events and organizational transactions hold in their lives. Their trust is based on the belief that the other person will relate to their frame of reference when viewing their activities and when puzzling through how organization events affect their personal chances for success. Sometimes these confidantes are adversaries in some organizational matter and in such instances each can count on the other to put energy into comprehending his or her position and to search for a course of action that does not push a pet project's success at the other's expense.

Not the least of the beneficiaries of such relationships is the organization. Trusting relationships based on respect for individual differences, are an important organizational resource. Most important, they enhance each individual's capacity to withstand challenge and confrontation, and to evaluate openmindedly an opinion or position that runs counter to his or her own. There are, in any large organization, an abundance of essential messages that either go unsent or are sent but not reasserted when the targeted person resists. Usually the challenger is not willing to risk losing the friendly relationship or, worse, risk retaliation. Such messages include most of the critical information and feedback an individual needs to hear in order to improve his or her skills and perspective and become successful. They involve justifications for programs that run counter to what the individual is currently working towards, criticisms based on positions that appear sympathetic to one's organization competitors, negative evaluations, and miscellaneous others the expression of which could do the organization a lot of good. Trusting relationships are the vehicles for cushioning such messages or, in certain instances, making sure they are sent before it becomes too late to rectify matters without causing damage either to the organization or to the individuals involved.

The Challenge

Managers know how important trusting relationships are to an organization and they have a preferred approach to getting them, which we call shared fate. However, once context is seen as the key ingredient of trust, the limitations of the shared fate approach become readily apparent. Shared fate works well in those situations where it is possible to capture the imagination and spirit of an entire organization unit behind a bona fide opportunity or threat. It works because it is effective in evoking commitment to a set of external goals whose primacy is such that, for the moment, self-commitments become secondary. Its limitations, however, result directly from the fact that individuals are rarely willing to subordinate their personal priorities indefinitely or even to postpone them for an extended period of time. For instance, a badly splintered British populus who formerly had rejected Winston Churchill's prewar leadership were easily able to unite behind him once they accepted the inevitability of actual conflict. Conversely, they were brutally quick in withdrawing their support and dumping the prime minister once the conflict had passed and the war effort was winding down.

The shared fate approach offers what probably appears to managers to be a shortcut where they can produce the effects of trust without exhibiting high levels of interpersonal skill. And this is convenient since most see the interpersonal processes associated with the creation of trusting relationships as more or less out of their control. But the shared fate approach is a shortcut that often creates strings of bottom-line measures and artificial crises with power politics—not trust—being the final result.

To us the shared fate approach is based on a premise of mutual dependency, not mutual understanding. And we see this as a weakness because it adds to the rationalistic expectation that, in the main, logic and objectivity will determine how organization events are decided. In contrast, the respect for individual differences approach emphasizes an understanding of what each of the parties has at stake in the situation and encourages people to acquire the skills to read these interests and to think about the need for context that accompanies them.

It is unlikely that the inclinations and preferences of managers will change much without a fundamental shift in how they think about organizations. Given the way the rationalistic model encourages managers to think, the shared fate approach is the best they seem able to do. The rational mind-set has a difficult time accepting the fact that *organizations do not exist independently of the subjective interests of those who comprise them*. It is naive to believe that six people can sit around a conference table and have an objective discussion of what goal structure best actualizes the needs of the firm without their own subjective interests playing a major role in what they ultimately conclude.

It is not that managers are either blind or dense. They know that subjectivity plays a major role in determining the outcome of organization events, but they lack a perspective that enables them to attach anything other than negative connotations to it. They are reluctant to acknowledge and legitimize the subjective element for fear that once the door is opened a crack they will be overwhelmed. They are afraid that an organization that deals explicitly with subjectivity will lose its objective component and run out of control. All of this poses serious obstacles to seeing the essential role that respect for individual differences can play in the development of trust and candid relationships at work.

SECTION II

Transacting with the Dominant Reality

IN THIS SECTION we present the theory that lies behind our radical perspective on people's needs for context, and the politics and trust issues that emanate from those needs. We explain the power struggles and the power politics that characterize organization life in attempt to make them more visible. For those who experience the stress but who are not sure of its cause, this section should be particularly instructive. It shows how mutable reality in an organization can be; it depicts the dilemmas that force people to endorse realities that they don't believe in personally; and it shows how individuals can assert themselves "strategically" when transacting with those who see reality differently than they see it.

Chapter 7 begins our presentation of theory with a description of how reality gets constructed in an organization. It describes how people negotiate subjective interests in constructing the reality that maximizes their chances of realizing what is personally important. It shows how the resulting reality is "objectified" and presented as the way things actually are. And it explains the dynamics that unfold when a reality that is accepted as "objective" fails to portray someone's projects and commitments in a favorable light.

Chapter 8 describes the basis of *power politics*—the embedding of one's personal and self-interested needs and perceptions in an advocacy that emphasizes what's good for the organization. It describes the *power struggles* sparked when people with different vested interests compete over definitions of the organization's reality. The stigma associated with subjectivity teaches people not to advocate based on personal need. Instead, people in organizations learn to preface what they say with ''The organization requires . . .''. This chapter describes how people with different needs transact with one another by camouflaging what is personally desirable and making a case for what the organization requires.

Chapter 9 contrasts the tactical and strategic approaches to organization politics and extends the discussion begun in Chapter 3. It describes the elements of the *strategic orientation* and how the strategic way of asserting oneself provides power and political leverage. It also describes the downside of using the tactical approach, particularly when operating in a forum in which one's words and actions can eventually become public knowledge.

CHAPTER 7

How Reality Is Constructed in an Organization

Up to this point we've been contending that most managers avoid the direct engagement of subjectivity out of the fear that doing so will open up more issues than they can handle. We've also been intimating that this is a head-in-the-sand approach. We see subjectivity as omnipresent and we see ways of engaging it directly that will not throw an organization out of control. A natural structure for constraining the subjective element is in effect. But if one does not see the structure, then for that person it does not exist, and expressions of subjectivity are experienced as threats to key managerial responsibilities such as maintaining discipline and exercising control. In this chapter we describe how the subjective element gives rise to what becomes institutionalized as the reality of an organization, and the processes that constrain deviations from what the power structure is willing to endorse. Our hope is that people who are presently apprehensive about dealing directly with the subjective element will use our model to take the next step towards a more integrated view and approach.

The Founder's Reality

In order to better understand the basis of reality in an organization and how each individual attempts to mold the organization's reality to fit with his or her unique needs for context, allow us to describe what might be called "the original organization event": two, three, four, or more people contemplating the founding of an organization. For the sake of simplicity, let's begin with them sitting in a room trying to decide how to exploit a business idea. What they contemplate often starts with externals such as thinking about what market opportunities exist and what way of organizing their efforts will take best advantage of a particular opportunity. Until they strike some key agreements, they're just a group of people spinning scenarios and holding a bull session while trying to predict the future. Once they reach an agreement about what they are going to produce, who is going to do what, and how individual efforts will be judged, they become an organization with an "objective" picture of reality. It is objective because everyone says he or she believes it to be true. Of course, constraining what each person agrees to are personal considerations which make that individual cognizant of what any particular scenario will do for him or her personally. Each person has a set of needs that must be satisfied before that person will lend his or her support to a particular portrayal of reality. In fact, to a large extent, the founding of an organization is an acknowledgement that people with differing and varied personal needs have created an overarching objective that allows their individual interests to fit well with one another.

Now that the organization has been founded, consider what makes it an "organization." In its essence, an organization is a group of people possessing different individual concerns and personal interests, but a common overarching objective or purpose, who have struck a set of agreements that lead them to see and interpret work-related events in a comparable manner. When something happens, or a certain set of circumstances occurs, each person attributes a comparable meaning and has a similar set of expectations about the kind of organization response that is required and whose job it is to do what. Some of these expectations are based more on rational concerns for the organization's effectiveness than on subjective interests. Some expectations are more personally motivated and subjective than rational. And, because the rational and subjective are so intertwined, most participants will not perceive the distinction between them.

Few people enter an organization at its founding. Most enter an ongoing operation and seek acceptance by buying into agreements that are already made. Usually they come with a set of needs compatible with what the founders had in mind so that the agreements they buy into do not significantly compromise what they believe or want. These people seek a meaningful relationship in which as many as possible of their personal needs can be fulfilled. Some minimum number of needs must be met or they will not join, and if some particular needs are not fulfilled, they either will not join or will join and participate duplicitously. And of course there is the need to have a relationship with this organization that is no worse than their best alternative.

Now imagine a newcomer entering the room with the original founders. First, he or she is told, "Here's how we see our situation and here's how we see your role." In response, the newcomer reflects on his or her own situation and ways of being effective and says, "I don't quite see it as you have laid it out for me." Mindful of the analysis, tough conversations, and negotiations the group went through in becoming an organization, the group spokesperson answers, "No, I'm afraid you don't understand. What you need to see are the following . . ." and then goes on to espouse the company line. The newcomer is presented with a set of assumptions that he or she was not present to hear discussed and which he or she must be persuaded, motivated, or coerced to accept. Of course, while many of these assumptions represent valid responses to external market conditions, many also represent accommodations to the needs of one or more founders. They are considerations that needed to be in the original contract in order for one or more of the founders to buy in. However, these accommodations are not stated as such—they are delivered as rational statements of what is "objectively" required.

For the sake of this example, let us say that the newcomer buys in, or at least says he or she does. Buying in will be based on what flexibility the newcomer sees for pursuing a version of the organization's reality that provides him or her with a job that has personal meaning and offers the opportunity to be a success, and the alternatives that person sees for a job somewhere else that will leave him or her better off.

In most organizations, newcomers, with their somewhat discrepant views of the organization's reality, eventually take responsible positions and wind up recruiting a second generation of newcomers who in turn wind up recruiting a third generation and so on. Thus, most established organizations are populated by people whose reasons for joining are less and less in harmony with the assumptions of the founders, and more and more based on what they see as flexibility in the prescribed ways of operating. This flexibility allows them to pursue functions and roles in ways that are personally meaningful to them. In fact, left to their own devices, most people attempt to modify the founders' reality in ways that emphasize and support what is personally and professionally important to them. Over time, significant changes and deviations in the founders' reality are institutionalized and a modified set of operating assumptions emerges.

With each generation the operating assumptions become more calcified and the latitudes for asserting personal interests become increasingly difficult to find. This is because there are more people who make the same assumptions and whose knee-jerk response is to stand up and set the newcomer straight. But the reality they are pushing is no longer that of the founders; it is an amalgam that no one in particular actually sees or wholly believes. It is an updated version of the assumptions people must make in their daily operations in order to demonstrate respect for a system that everyone has already agreed to go along with. This reality serves as a constraint on each individual's inclination to pursue his or her self-interests without adequate regard for what others assert are the interests of the organization.

The Dominant Reality

We use the term *dominant reality* to describe the new operating assumptions that are worked out over time. It is the "how do they do it here?" reality that newcomers search out in order to fit in and feel secure. Like the founders' reality, the dominant reality directs daily operations by providing a common frame of reference to which everybody in the organization can relate. It provides the standards that people can use in arbitrating their individual differences and in achieving an integrated approach to operating the organization. Like the founders' reality, it specifies what is going to be produced, how production is to be accomplished, who has what role in producing it, what constitutes contribution, and how contributions will be assessed and rewarded. *Unlike* the founders' reality, it remains separate from what is believed by any individual, although any given aspect may overlap what particular individuals think.

The dominant reality directs relations within the firm by specifying the values, expectations, and assumptions that people who make up the organization are supposed to hold. It also directs relations with people outside the firm by specifying the basic premises that underlie the conduct of the organization's business. It provides guidelines for representing the organization's products and services, for identifying target customers and clients, for characterizing the organization's position in the marketplace, and for deciding how products and services are to be marketed and promoted.

The dominant reality provides a tangible constraint that people can use in limiting the individualistic aspects of their thinking and performance. It serves as a control against blatantly self-interested interpretations of organizational events and the inclination to exploit each organizational event for one's own personal success. In short, the dominant reality provides order in what otherwise would be a highly idiosyncratic interplay of individual beliefs and actions and it provides the grounds for people to hold each other accountable.

The dominant reality provides for people who have different attitudes, values, and ethics the ability to galvanize themselves around common business practices and relationship codes. For instance, some organizations value and promote team players who create the conditions for others to contribute; others promote star performers. Some organizations require careful portrayals of the entire truth when dealing with clients and customers; others promote glossing over potential problem areas and not mentioning the possibility of a problem until it materializes. The dominant reality presents guidelines for all of this and more.

In providing a common frame of reference, the dominant reality gives people a language for exchanging their individual perceptions. Without it organizations would be Towers of Babel and would run out of control. People would relate to the same events on different dimensions and use different words with different meanings. Without a common language there would be virtually no efficiency of effort, for people would have no way to build on one another's contributions or to link to the contributions of those who came before them.

Without the dominant reality there would be his reality and her reality. With it, there is his reality, her reality, and the reality that they both accept. The third, or accepted reality may or may not be one that has validity to either of the people involved, but is the most important reality because it is the one that each will publicly use in relating to the other's behavior and in "fairly" evaluating what that person contributes.

Because the pressures to have it are considerable, the dominant reality takes on an existence of its own. We have already discussed how it is presented to newcomers, and those who weren't in the room when key agreements were struck. It is presented as a set of "objective" facts and not mere operating givens. Many of its underlying assumptions were conceived at a previous point in time and under different market conditions and by people who long ago left the company, whose personal needs are no longer a relevant consideration. But talking about these assumptions with an air of objectivity, as if they were shibboleths and absolutes, makes these changed conditions difficult to detect. Thus, extant dominant realities take on an existence of their own, with people talking about what "objectively" exists rather than what has been merely "agreed to" and thus could be changed.

Sometimes the dominant reality is the result of power politics whereby people with rank assert their will on those lower down. For instance, a great deal of discussion and heated debate may precede a decision about what a department or work unit ought to produce and who has what role in the production. And often the decision is not what anyone who has to implement it independently believes it should be. It's a decision that must be accepted because people with rank expressed the intensity of what they thought and wanted. But after the decision is made, what is to be produced will be accepted as fact, and people who initially disagreed with the role they are now expected to play understand that their evaluation will be based on what others feel entitled to expect.

Most often, however, the dominant reality is the result of give-and-take compromise hit upon as people with different self-interests struggle to decide the meaning that events hold for themselves and others. What gets agreed to and accepted as fact is worked out when a critical number of people, or one or more key people with power, uncover a definition of reality that does enough for what their self-interested perceptions tell them is in the organization's interests. Sometimes people are genuinely swayed by the discussion and adopt the group's conclusion as their own perception. But more often, people compromise and concede. What they now assert as reality is not totally the result of what they actually think or believe needs to be done. It is at least partially the result of their needs to get along, be accepted, or earn a credit for use on an issue of greater personal importance. Or their agreement may be the result of a recognition that to hold out and not go along would allow others to portray them as an obstacle to the organization's progress. In fact, a group's decision may not be what any individual thinks is organizationally correct; it may merely be the best set of agreements that those who participate think they can reach at the time.

Oftentimes the dominant reality is the result of political agreements struck by people whose different but overlapping motives lead them to agree to describe organizational happenings in a certain way, and whose projects and personal interests are furthered by getting others to agree with their descriptions. Thus, to our way of seeing things, a dominant reality is a construction of political expediency and not a reality that has its origins in consensual belief. The origins are in personally convenient compromises that appear to fit in with the needs of the people agreeing to them. Consensual belief is a phenomenon that may or may not take place after an agreement about the nature of reality is struck.

In practice, however, even those who were present when compromise agreements (about the nature of the organization's reality) were struck talk as if a reality exists that actually reflects how things are. This way of talking and thinking gives internal stability to an organization. If people were to act otherwise, and to speak as if what was accepted as operationally valid were arbitrary and the result of personal expediency, they would be opening a big can of worms. All agreements would be seen as variables open for rediscussion and no decision could be counted on to last with any permanence. Each decision would be vulnerable to unlimited debate and issues of power and self-convenience would be blatantly visible. This is much too much for today's organization mind to tolerate and would produce great upheaval and personal insecurity. Thus, to a great extent, everyone talks about the organization's reality as if it were fixed and more or less permanent—as if it were a consensual belief.

Each organization has its own dominant reality complete with rationales that people can use in justifying what they advocate. Theorists have referred to these as "reconstructed logics" and "ideas in good currency." People use these rationales to justify their decisions in the same way that lawyers use previous court decisions to support what they assert. However, unlike the law, organizations do not require consistency or precedent. Which precedent is to be followed and which should be conveniently forgotten, which rule can be bent, which line of the business plan may be overlooked—all these are options of the people involved and subject to what others, acting on their own values and self-interests, decide to let them get away with.

The dominant reality contains "categories," and once people learn to identify them, they become determining factors in how people relate to work events. It's analogous to watching Olympic figure skating and finding out that judges separate technical skills and artistry of performances. All of a sudden one finds oneself viewing subsequent performances with new standards and new criteria for appreciation. In this way categories give people their bearings. In an organization, personal thoughts and one's experience of events are merely fragments of one's perception and personal reality until they are referenced in dimensions that the group has agreed are important in the monitoring of these events. Only then do they become part of one's organization experience. In one company its' servicing the customer, in another it's protecting cash and maintaining liquidity, and in a third it's gaining market share. It's within these categories that one makes sense of one's own role in the organization's response.

Organizations not only provide categories but they also provide standards, directions, and ideals which the individual can use in evaluating what an event means to the organization and what specific happenings signify for the accomplishment of organizational goals. In other words, an organization relies on its members to reference their experience in a similar set of categories and to develop a shared sense of what state within each category signifies a desirable situation and what poses a threat. In fact, we would go so far as to assert that a collection of people only becomes an organization when they subject their personal experiences to a comparable set of categories with similar value positions and standards. Conversely, the greatest threat to an organization arises when key members reference their experiences in different categories, or within the same category but using different values or standards to evaluate them.

Just as the organization needs constraints to protect itself against any one individual's personal reality running out of control, so the organization needs constraints to keep its person-made dominant reality from getting out of control. For most organizations at least two such constraints exist. The first is the people who consume the organization's product and/or the marketplace in which the organization conducts its business; the second is the people who currently manage and staff the organization and/or who are available in the professional and labor markets to replace them. Together these groups act as forces that prevent the organization's reality from becoming too arbitrary or capricious. Organizations with a reality that has gotten too far out of control lose their ability to relate to customers and lose their ability to attract capable employees. Of course organizations with captive market-places or with captive labor pools are able to forge realities that indulge those who presently control the organization at the expense of consumers or of their own personnel, and when their indulgences become too extreme it's up to government or labor unions to step in and force a better balance.

We have asserted that the dominant reality is a reality of agreements negotiated by founders and amended by successive generations of organizational participants. It is the result of people attempting to modify organizational givens to produce a definition of reality which characterizes the organization's interests in a way that maximizes the expression of their own. Of course one's own interests also include the organization's viability in the market-place, competent people to staff the organization, compliance with government regulations, and so on.

The dominant reality is also a reality of compromise, one that will satisfy a collection of people who together possess a critical mass of organization power. It is not necessarily a reality that accurately reflects how anyone in particular actually sees organization events. It is a reality that reflects what people with varying positions of power have agreed to or that, because of other issues of high personal priority, they are willing to go along with, or one that because of lack of power, they simply cannot do anything about. Our point of view contrasts with the more commonly advanced view that, in an organization, reality is consensually arrived at, reflecting a set of perceptions in which most people genuinely believe. Certainly this is what the founders are often able to achieve with one another. However, most people are not founders and many founders, such as individual entrepreneurs, never succeed in getting their reality internalized by anyone else. In our model, in fact, no single individual may actually see an issue exactly as it is defined by official organization policy, and the organizational view that is expressed today merely represents a set of compromises that may get reworked tomorrow.

The Individual's Dilemma

Working in an organization is tantamount to living with two realities. The first is the reality of the individual and what he or she truly believes exists. The second is the operating reality of the organization, which we call the dominant reality. Each of these realities produces its own world, a world that can differ significantly depending on the individual and the circumstances. And it is precisely these differences, differences between the dominant reality of the organization and the reality of the individual, that reduce an individual's power in the organization and establish his or her need to acquire more.

Our work in organizations has taught us that an individual's power is maximized when the gap between his or her personal reality and the reality of the organization is minimal. Then others can easily understand the basis for his or her actions and what he or she says makes instant organizational sense. Conversely, the least powerful position is to have one's private reality at odds with mainstream assumptions and be in the situation where one is constantly faced with defending the value of what he or she does.

This is not to say that an individual's power is totally determined by the ability to tailor his or her reality to the dominant reality at work. Certainly one's role, responsibilities, and personal abilities are key factors in determining an individual's power. But we have found that the efficiency of an individual's words and actions goes up considerably to the extent that the assumptions that underlie what that individual sees and believes are compatible with assumptions that are mainstream. One merely has to state a personal point of view and others can easily reference it in current images and ideology. One has merely to make a motion and others will understand its intent and comprehend the organization logic behind it.

Being in sync with the dominant reality provides people with feelings of strength and well-being. One can readily state what is on one's mind with confidence that those who think differently will have to justify the framework beneath their opposing belief before gaining sufficient credibility to advance their point of view. Being in sync with the dominant reality also gives an individual tremendous latitude in ignoring or dismissing out of hand perspectives that go against what he or she advocates.

Of course most people start a job with a personal reality that has some significant differences from that which is mainstream in their new organization. As soon as these differences are recognized, the individual's options in the struggle for personal power become more clear. One can learn more about the operating assumptions of the organization and attempt to reshape oneself in images that conform to mainstream organizational beliefs. Or, one can attempt to anchor oneself in the image that makes greatest personal sense, in the belief that this will also lead to the most organizational effectiveness, and adopt a strategy of lying in wait for timely opportunities to convert others to one's way of seeing reality and formulating events.

While in practice most people make significant accommodations to what they experience as the mainstream organizational reality, most people, most of the time, also seek to change the organization's reality to place it in greater harmony with their own personal needs for context. Often this is seen as a struggle for raw power. In our minds it's a struggle for power all right, but the goal is not raw power at the expense of others. The goal is personal power, and the struggle is to establish the conditions that allow an individual with unique needs for context to be effective in an organization that has a preexisting and different reality.

CHAPTER 8

Power Transactions

In the last chapter we saw that personal power can result from having needs for context that parallel realities that are mainstream in the organization. We saw that the most powerful people are those possessing a *founder's reality*; we saw that the next most powerful people are those who are fortunate enough to find a significant overlap between their needs for context and what, through agreements, has been established as the *dominant reality*. We also observed that few people who lack such overlap want to submit to the conformity that comes from artificially reshaping themselves to fit within an established and prespecified dominant reality. Instead they seek to acquire more power by reshaping that reality. Of course others resist; thus every organizational event becomes an opportunity for conflict, domination, and power struggles. This chapter examines the transactions that arise as people with different needs for context vie with one another over what form the dominant reality should take.

In order to see the constant and dynamic interplay between people and their attempts to reshape the dominant reality, we begin with the individual. In an organization, each individual has a dual obligation. He or she must find an orientation that makes personal sense, and gravitate towards those tasks that are personally meaningful and that he or she believes must be accomplished by someone in his or her role and position. At the same time he or she must orient to that which has been agreed upon as important and constituting the dominant reality of the organization. The presence of this duality creates the need to exploit every event and to make a response that is in a form that both the individual and others can value.

Success for people who fail at either is problematic. The individual who compromises his or her personal reality and incorporates too much of what has been labeled "valid" by the organization quickly loses his or her unique identity and, we would argue, loses the core of his or her value to the organization. Such an individual is stuck asking others the meaning of events and eventually becomes encapsulated in an outdated picture of the organization's reality. Conversely, an individual who orients primarily to realities that are anchored in his or her personal picture of reality lacks the ability to learn from others with different points of view and loses touch with the marketplaces in which the organization conducts its business. Eventually that person's contributions begin to look disconnected from that which others perceive as organizationally valid and/or market-relevant.

Likewise, organizations themselves experience negative consequences from having either too much or too little conformity—from having a dominant reality that either is quite fixed and rigid or, at the other extreme, quite open to change by individuals pursuing a self-beneficial cause. The organization with a fixed picture of reality extracts such conformity from its people, not just in actions but in perception, that it loses its ability to adjust to changes in customer needs and to social and economic forces in the marketplace, and suffers a declining business. And, organizations that are too open to influence become political nightmares with people openly lobbying for flagrantly self-beneficial and disconnected interpretations of the dominant reality.

Fortunately, most organizations fall somewhere in the middle. Thus, while people exert pressure to modify and change the dominant reality, most of these pressures come from well-intentioned individuals who are also looking to make the organization more effective. They attempt to reconcile potential conflicts between their self-interests and the organization's well-being by adopting an orientation that simultaneously seeks a "win" for themselves and a "win" for the organization. That is, people relate to but a subset of the actions that could advance, improve, and produce a "win" for the organization—the subset that also enhances their chances of producing a "win" for themselves, however that win is personally defined. What's more, most people usually attempt to postpone or sacrifice the satisfaction of personal needs that come at what they perceive to be the organization's expense. Our shorthand terminology for an orientation that seeks outcomes that are simultaneously both organizationally and personally productive is "win-win." This contrasts with the "win-lose" approach that arises when people advance either the organization's or their own interests at the expense of the other.

Developing a "win-win" approach presents people with a structural puzzle. Until solved, it's a puzzle that hampers one's every action, as the individual must take time to reflect back and forth about how doing for the organization can be good for him- or herself, or how doing for him- or herself benefits the organization. Solving this puzzle provides an orientation that shows the individual the connection between what he or she is doing and its value for the organization. The person who understands this connection operates with a spontaneity that brings *personal power*. And to the extent that this orientation overlaps the dominant reality of the organization and is acknowledged as valid by others, that person achieves *organizational power* as well.

A win-win approach entails a selective valuing of the dominant reality. For example, if, hypothetically speaking, there are 11,643 dimensions to the dominant reality, an individual will strive to emphasize those 317 that best reflect what that person has at stake individually and self-interestedly. And he or she will seek modifications in those 42 that, in their modified form, would best support that person's needs for personal and organizational context.

Inevitably, people with different win-win approaches will conflict in what they advance, oppose, and emphasize in the way of organizational directions. Of course all that is advocated will be justified on the grounds of what benefits or hinders the organization. But such justifications are only partially valid, for the connections between what an individual states and his or her self-interested reasons for stating it are hidden. Such explanations protect advocates from being seen as pushing personally convenient perceptions without consideration for the organization's welfare.

Thus, on a daily basis, organization debates are carried out on an "objective" level, with people arguing the pros and cons of what's best for the organization without mentioning their personal attachments to the directions they advocate. And the point of departure is usually the dominant reality. An individual may seek to modify it, add to it, or make a basic change in the course of discussions about which facets of the dominant reality are higher order, are more timely, create more of an opportunity, are more essential, constitute a better use of resources, are more efficient, and so on. In essence, people negotiate the emphasis of various facets of the dominant reality and seek to amend it without revealing the personal considerations that underlie their inclination and advocacy.

There are many levels to the personally convenient modifications and changes that people propose in the dominant reality. Certainly there is the level of an individual trying to make the organization more profitable and effective, which also adds to the image and security of each person who is a part of that work effort. At another level, an individual may seek changes in the way his or her department is valued inside the organization, which also enhances his or her status and perceived value. At yet another level, an individual may seek changes that call attention to the unique contribution he or she makes to the success of a completed project. In any event, one's motives are intertwined with the adjustments one advocates.

Transacting with Others

Whether or not an individual has clear sailing in changing a dominant reality depends on what the change he or she advocates implies for others and the extent of their needs to have the organization's reality remain as it is. There are many reasons why people resist attempts to change what is considered to be the dominant reality, and, unfortunately, holding out for the "truth" is not usually one of them. We wish we could say it was; life would be simpler that way. But we've seen too many instances of organizations calling an "apple" an "orange" and pursuing their distorted definition as long as the marketplace would let them get away with it. Such was the case when Detroit automakers went through a long period of holding out for and promoting large cars with more chrome—thus denying both the public's needs to conserve gas and get value in return for the higher prices they were paying and the companys' needs to sell cars and keep foreign imports from eating up their markets.

Those who propose organizational change should take care not to be lulled into thinking that the dominant reality is an accurate depiction of what exists; they should remember that it is the result of compromise. They should understand that no matter how sound the organizational rationale they espouse, others who sense their own personal situations worsening will feel the need to oppose them. On the other hand, most proposals to change the organization's reality will benefit at least some others and most proposers seek these people out, identify the features that hold appeal for them (which often are different from what appeals to the proposer), and enlist their support for the change. Sometimes it is possible to frame one's appeal at the time of the initial conversation and pose it, on-line, for group acceptance. Most of the time, however, the correct phrasing takes time and inquiry. Opinion leaders who have vested interests in what is being changed must be consulted and the appeal and modifications in what has been proposed must be implicitly worked out with them prior to going public and making one's organization pitch.

In an organization, the prototypical power transaction takes place when two people interact on a proposed reality adjustment whose outcome matters to both. For example, they might disagree on directions for a new product line, the structure for staffing a new project, the format for conducting a program review, how to spend the training budget, what categories belong on the new evaluation form—almost any topic that directly or indirectly impacts their individual needs for context. Usually both are pushing for a resolution or subset of organizational modifications that produces a win for themselves and a win for the organization, and usually each is limited by the need to find a win-win that the other will permit. If the two should hit upon a reality construction that fits both of their needs, then they will probably agree. But if they cannot find a mutually satisfying construction, then they have a problem, the seriousness of which varies with the stakes the participants attach to the outcome. Usually this is a competitive situation because only on the rarest of occasions can the situation be defined as the search for a *win-win-win*, with the third win being a reality adjustment that provides the other person what he or she desires in the way of context.

The dynamics of a two-person reality construction change dramatically once the participants find themselves unable to produce simultaneous win-wins (this differs from win-win-wins). At this point the participants are likely to extend their competition to a level where their power struggle is more obvious. They begin to engage in head-to-head competition. But before acting out their competition they reflect on the longer-term costs associated with going into combat and with winning or losing. They reflect, "Do I really want to fight with this person?" The participants switch from a purely tactical approach to one that is more strategic.

Up to this point the participants were merely debating the pros and cons of the organizational "improvements" they each sought to make—with the intensity of effort attached to their arguments at least somewhat a reflection of the personal stakes they attach to the issue at hand. But given an impasse, what they have at stake personally expands to include the relationship they have with the other and the implications this potential dispute holds for their entire role in the system. Said more concretely, an individual worries about such factors as the consequences of arguing with a boss who appears to make each fight a test of his or her authority and who seems to have an overwhelming need to be right; likewise, an individual worries about the consequences of not arguing with a boss whose critical point of view, if unchecked, could spell trouble for one's organizational role, value, and credibility. Simply said, there are times when, for strategic reasons, one can't afford the luxury of winning a power struggle, and there are times when the consequences associated with conceding it are disastrous and when an individual must take a stand to his or her "organizational death".

While the prototypical power transaction is two people looking to maximize their own positions while debating the organization's interests, by no means should this be taken as all there is to their debate. Usually others are involved too, and their participation becomes apparent once the time comes to implement what the two decide. That is, two people may agree on an element of an organization's reality but usually that element is subject to broader ratification prior to its incorporation as part of the dominant reality. And once those who are impacted by the construction get wind of it, they can be counted on to make their interests known.

And how they do so depends on the organizational forums available to them.

People who have a need to control, influence, or change a dominant organization reality, or to influence someone else's proposal to modify a dominant reality, inevitably find ways to make their perspectives known. In fact, nowhere is creativity more apparent in an organization than in the ways people find for inserting their needs and interests into organizational discussions. People tell calculated versions of what they believe to be the truth, frame problems to feature self-convenient opportunities, release reports and information at personally opportune times, play to the point of view of power figures who can help them, concede on certain issues in order to win an obligation for help at another time, cultivate organizationally convenient relationships, and we could go on and on. All of these political tactics are aimed at creating a dominant reality that is congruent with one's self-interests and needs for context.

Few organizations give explicit thought to creating the forums that allow people to pursue self-interested advocacies in a forthright manner. We say this despite the fact that everyone has regularly scheduled meetings with the people they need to influence—task force information exchanges, weekly management group meetings, supervisory sessions, reviews of the business plan, and the like—but seldom are the critical topics discussed directly. Most often these topics are raised obliquely, behind the scenes, as people find an endless number of ways to feed in information aimed at getting others to see the world in a way that is compatible with their interests. Always the goal is to create a context that is friendly to one's orientation, and because the lobby is indirect and the motives are hidden, the process is considered political. Involved are what we call power politics.

It's easy for people to tell when they are directly involved in a power transaction or a politicized situation, for how they inwardly experience organization events will be at odds with the dominant reality in which they feel they must communicate. On the other hand, it's more difficult to see one's involvement in a power transaction when the political dynamics are caused by the bind someone *else* finds him- or herself in. Then, the discrepant experience resides inside that someone else and the only telling clues are momentary hesitations in that other person's spontaneity. Nevertheless, someone who is sensitive to the existence of the organization's reality can sense when politics are in the air by noticing that the dominant reality is making it very difficult for an individual or a group of individuals to succeed. That is, organizations are political to the extent that the dominant reality favors people with certain needs and interests and discriminates against people with other needs and interests. The out-of-favor group, or person, finds its success and even its survival tied to changing the dominant reality. Then, every organizational happening becomes an opportunity to pursue change by whatever tactical means are available, which others usually experience as politically initiated action.

It's far easier to think about what might depoliticize an organizational situation than to actually take action that does so. Politics are less necessary once an individual succeeds in getting others to acknowledge the validity of his or her needs for personal context—in terms of this chapter, to seek win-win-wins. However, making the third win part of one's personal orientation often entails a sacrifice of organizational power. It is necessary to take serious account of someone else's contrasting and opposing points of view and to let that person know that one is doing so. Such a strategy runs counter to sound practices of hard-line advocacy and is often cited as the key problem that hampered Carter-era Democrats and the United States position in world politics at the time. Instead of making his pitch on simple "truths" and declarative "win-win" statements of reality, Jimmy Carter and his administration's diplomats acknowledged the presence of multiple realities and conflicting interests, and proposed strategies which, in their respect for the opposition, compromised the power and forcefulness of their own advocacy. In acknowledging the rationality of their competitors' interests they increased the responsibility of the United States to a point where they found it much easier to react to another country's exclusion of U.S. interests than to assert a coherent viewpoint of their own.

Organizations prosper when their members adopt win-win-win approaches that explicitly take into account the context needs of those with whom they interact. However, doing so compromises the effectiveness of an individual's self-advocacy and, at least in the short run, seems to come at the expense of that person's organizational power. Hence, each individual has a dilemma: whether to take the competitive win-win approach that maximizes one's short-run effectiveness and organizational power, or to take the "other-responsive" win-win-win approach that makes the organization effective. Clearly more people would choose the latter if they knew ways of doing so that did not come at great personal expense.

CHAPTER 9

Assuming the Strategic Orientation

We've examined the processes that shape an organization's reality; we're now ready to be more definitive in our characterization of the *strategic orientation* and the skills required to implement it. In particular, we are interested in how an individual can assume the strategic orientation in engaging the competitive and political forces that result from others taking a win-win approach. These are the forces that shape and control the dominant reality and ultimately determine whether or not an organization becomes internally effective.

Our readers will recall the discussion at the end of Chapter 3 in which we drew a dichotomy between the tactical and strategic orientations. We depicted the tactical as the orientation in which people become so preoccupied with their own immediate needs for context that they extend very little concern for another person's context needs or point of view, except as it represents support or opposition for their own. We depicted the *strategic* as the orientation that seeks context from relationships. The strategic orientation directs people not simply to vie for interpretations of events that support their own needs for context, but to concern themselves with building the types of relationships in which other people are motivated to put them in the proper context and have the information to do so. Chapter 3 also mentioned the importance of showing respect for the context needs of others and taking what we are now calling a win-win-win approach.

There is, however, another distinguishing feature of the strategic orientation, one that we have not yet emphasized sufficiently. This has to do with the importance of operating from a position of strength and not allowing others to neglect one's interests while one is showing consideration for theirs. Respecting another person and building a relationship should not mean neglecting one's own interests or putting them on hold for an indefinite period of time. One should be able to comprehend another person's framework and show respect for it without sacrificing the ability to assert oneself.

Symbolic Events

The contrast between strategic and tactical orientations becomes particularly vivid when one understands the existence and nature of *symbolic events*. In daily organization life there exist particularly sensitive moments when a small incident becomes all-important and powerful because people treat it as indicative of an entire system and predictive of things to come. An event has symbolic significance when it is interpreted as having broader and more general implications for one or more of the principal parties involved.

The impact of a symbolic event is created by the significance that key others attach to a particular occurrence which may or may not have a direct connection to the subject being addressed. For instance, we remember an incident where a mistake in seating assignments put a political outcast at the table next to the chairman of the board at the company's annual management briefing. This resulted in the widespread perception that the outcast had been readmitted to the "inner circle." And, every four years we are treated to a host of symbolic events radiating from presidential primaries when what takes place in the Grange Halls of New Hampshire is flashed across the media as if it were to have telltale significance for the American voting populus as a whole.

Symbolic events are moments when specific actions and behaviors are read more as a sign of things to come than for their literal impact on the case at hand. For instance, when a new boss takes over a division, everybody watches him or her intently until the first few transfers, firings, and promotions have occurred.

Similarly, in the management classroom, professors are scrutinized for their standards, and their ways of dealing with inadequately thought-out comments or wrong answers are interpreted as representative of how they deal with all situations, not just the specific instance being observed.

There are no absolute guidelines for designating which events receive symbolic attributions: what turns out to be symbolic depends on the issues that are central in an onlooker's mind and what idiosyncratic meanings are tied to what that onlooker sees and hears. As in instances involving a new boss or new professor, the absence of solid information regarding the authority's intentions leads onlookers to scan each small event for clues that forecast things to come. Unlike these instances, however, predicting exactly which events are likely to be perceived symbolically, and the dimensions on which they will be read, requires knowledge of the individuals involved and an ability to anticipate the emotions that specific situations evoke in them.

Individuals interpret events symbolically when they perceive them to play a decisive role in determining how the "system" operates in relation to them or in deciding key facets of their image and credibility. This is why certain moments and performances take on such paramount significance and become major pressures in an individual's life. For instance, consider the stakes and the emotions that were stimulated when, in a well-attended staff meeting, a male manager "innocuously" asked the newly hired female MBA assistant, "While you're up, please get me a cup of coffee, *dear*."

We could write volumes on the variety of emotions and interpretations this "simple" request evoked, for the story of what took place will be repeated many times before the incident is forgotten. However, in terms of the present discussion it is instructive to focus on the tactical and strategic considerations involved in the assistant's response to the "Get me a cup of coffee, dear" request. Simultaneously, this woman was concerned with getting through the moment with her professional identity and self-esteem intact, with putting her relationship with the man making the request on respectful terms, and with establishing her relationship with everyone else in the company, whether they were in or out of the room.

As it happened, this woman responded tactically. She asserted her identity at the expense of the relationships. Loudly and clearly

she said, ''Sorry, Milt, but getting coffee is *not* part of my job.''
Everyone else noticed that Milt's chair was pinned in a corner
where he had no easy access to the coffee-maker. And the people
who had been around knew Milt to be among the least chauvinis-
tic men on the staff, understood he was not testing her, and realized that he had thrown in the ''dear'' as a humorous signal that
he was sensitive to the potential stereotype, and was merely asking a favor.

Of course the ''Sorry, Milt'' response was tactical. Susan, the
assistant, was overly defensive about the possibility of being
treated as a ''go-for'' and had chosen this moment as the opportunity to defend her identity and assert her professionalism. Milt
apologized, but Susan's stridency cost her, and at least temporarily labeled her as overly sensitive and aggressive. Many people got
to know her better and moved beyond that first impression. A
couple of them tease her good-naturedly about it still. But others
never got beyond that impression and in turn dealt defensively
with Susan, which set up the conditions for her to respond in
kind. Those relationships are still tense, four months later. Happily the relationship with Milt was rectified quickly. Milt is an
easygoing guy and Susan, reflecting on her aggressiveness, was
only too happy for the opportunity to reconcile.

Most symbolic events occur spontaneously without key participants having a chance to prepare themselves to make a strategic
response. If, in the preceding instance, Susan had had the luxury
of calling ''time out'' and then had gathered more data on Milt
and on how others were viewing her in this situation, we're confident she would have made a strategic response. Knowing Susan,
she probably would have figured out some humorous way to
simultaneously assert her professionalism and build her relationship with the group. The problem was that Susan was on the spot
and felt she had no choice but to make an immediate response.
Feeling on the defensive, she responded tactically.

In our experience, most people engage symbolic events on a
tactical level. People find the immediate stakes associated with the
moment so compelling that their inclination to maximize the
present is sharply reinforced. They therefore adopt an overly robust attitude that assumes they can cope with the aftermath of
their strong response later on. Along these lines, we're constantly
reminding people that the real topic being discussed is their relationship with the person with whom they are arguing, and that

the specific subject has importance primarily for how its outcome affects future issues between them. Of course, people understand this without our telling them, but they get so embroiled in the moment that they need reminding.

We hope our discussion of Susan's situation demonstrates that we are sympathetic to people who feel pressured to assume the tactical orientation, but we abhor the interpersonal dynamics and organizational situations that are created in their wake. People operate tactically out of circumstance, force of habit, and a lack of superior alternatives. They have an immediate need for context that is so acute that they simply lose the capacity to attend to their relationships and the context needs of others. Moreover, the tactical can become so ingrained as a way of operating that people create prisons for themselves that sharply limit their ability to influence organization events constructively and noncompetitively. Their participation becomes a hopelessly political force in the lives of those with whom they interact.

The Strategic Response

The radical management perspective alerts us to at least three of the skills required for an individual to operate strategically without incurring undue vulnerability.

1. An individual must possess a strong sense of his or her strengths and organization value, and understand the minimum conditions required for him or her to operate effectively.

2. An individual must have the ability to communicate his or her strengths and associated needs for context so that others can comprehend what he or she has to contribute and what supporting role he or she can play.

3. An individual must possess the ability to perceive another person's strengths accurately and be responsible to his or her needs for context in key organizational situations.

With these skills in mind, review with us two instances where managers were able to make use of their understanding of symbolic events to operate more strategically. Both illustrate the use of the strategic orientation in engaging the competitive and political forces set in motion by others using a tactical approach.

The first instance involves an army brigadier general with responsibilities for coordinating the annual Pentagon budget proposal. In confiding to us the secret of his success, the general described his experience as follows:

> When I first took over as Director of Army Budgets I was faced with a structure that was guaranteed to be adversarial. Key commanders and division directors arrived at the appointed meeting place with an entourage of staff and, when the time came for them to speak, they would make the most partisan case for their unit's budget needs. Nothing I could say was useful in getting commanders to make the necessary concessions for putting together a budget that was realistic for the Army as a whole. And, as the most junior ranking officer in the room, I was certainly in no position to single-handedly cut a unit commander's budget request.
>
> Then I had an insight. I figured I could make more headway by breaking the process into two distinct steps. The first followed tradition and brought together all of the major bureau directors and their key staffs to hear each chief give a hell-fire presentation of his unit's essential projects and funding needs.
>
> For the second step, we excused all the adjutants and let them run back to their units with stories of how the "old man," their commander or bureau director, took a hard line and didn't concede an inch. This allowed each of the principals to maintain his image. Of course, with their staffs gone, the dynamics changed dramatically. The game changed from hard-ball advocacy to producing an integrated budget that would fly with the Congress.

The general was sensitive to the fact that the public meetings in which each unit's budget needs were put forward served as a symbolic event in which each commander had to demonstrate the forcefulness with which he could portray his unit's story to the wider bureaucracy. Rather than fight this tradition, the general acknowledged its validity and added a second step where the audience switched from one's unit to one's peers. Correspondingly, the symbolic issue shifted from demonstrating fierce loyalty to one's unit to demonstrating loyalty to the Army as a whole. From the standpoint of the three skills necessary for a strategic response, the General utilized the third brilliantly by reading the commanders' needs for context and developing a process that was responsive to them.

Our next illustration highlights the remaining two skills that are necessary for a strategic orientation: the importance of being clear in one's own mind about the conditions one needs to operate with strength, and the ability to communicate these conditions and associated needs for context to others. Such abilities are particularly useful in operating strategically, even when faced with the challenge of symbolic events which require an immediate on-line response.

This story involves a newly hired manager's efforts to establish himself in the early days following his joining a chief executive's staff.

Bob had been brought in to fill a vacancy in the top advisory group reporting to the president. Shortly after he assumed the position, he sent the president a memo outlining what he saw as his areas of responsibility and his first impressions of the directions he needed to take. When, after ten days, he got no response he called over to headquarters and asked the president's chief aide, "What's the status of my memo?" And when the aide replied, "To be real honest with you, Bob, he hasn't seen it yet; we decided it wasn't high-priority enough to send in right away," Bob hit the roof!

Shouting into the phone, Bob said, "Listen you sonofabitch, I don't care whether you write on the cover 'Here's another crazy memo from Bob' or 'This memo is crap,' but when I send a memo over for the president's attention, I want it sent in to him. The next time I hear it isn't, I'm either going to resign or get you thrown out of there or both. Do you understand me?"

In actuality this story is not about just any manager trying to get the attention and focus of any president but about Robert Strauss in his early days as a cabinet-level appointee in the Carter administration. On the surface, it would seem very risky for most of us to do what Robert Strauss did. In Strauss's case it might not have been. We suspect that he had run into comparable situations before, and when he saw the pattern developing again he instantly knew what to do—declare it a symbolic event and assert himself. In his mind, whatever value he was going to have would come from providing broader political counsel than President Carter had previously received, and this meant deep involvement in the president's everyday affairs. His function was to advise the president on political posturing in all matters of state, so access was the minimal condition he needed.

Strauss read the White House staffer's response as a clear-cut indication that access was going to be a problem. It is possible that he overreacted a bit, but we don't think so. He was not being treated as a person who had been called in halfway into Carter's first term in office to help a president with severe image problems, badly in need of political advice. The aide was not discriminating. In the fraction of a second it took Strauss to deduce this, he chose to make that phone conversation a major test of his ability to establish a preferential relationship with the president.

Central in his strategic handling of this situation was, first and foremost, Strauss's ability to see clearly the minimal conditions required for him to play an effective role as presidential counselor. The second skill that gave Strauss's response a strategic quality was his ability to articulate his context needs on the spot in a clear and forceful fashion. Together these skills set the stage for Robert Strauss to become one of Jimmy Carter's most trusted advisors, a role he played throughout the president's final two years in office.

From external appearances it seems Strauss neglected the third skill for operating strategically: being responsive to the other person's needs for context. He appeared to steam-roller over the White House staffer's context needs, pinning that person between the proverbial rock and hard place. But in fact Strauss did understand the aide's role in prioritizing the president's workload and disagreed with the priority assigned to him. Being sensitive to another person's needs should never be interpreted as synonymous with becoming a slave to them. Above all, operating strategically entails creating a stable structure for operating effectively over time. And that is what Strauss did. With laser-like precision, he put his issue on the table and declared the minimal terms of his participation.

Asserting oneself, as Strauss did, often leaves behind people harboring a grudge, looking for an opportunity for revenge. Strauss knew this and counted on the fact that, given the opportunity to work closely with the White House staffer, he would be able to compensate for any bad impression caused by his sharp-tongued approach. The fact that they both worked together for two years leads us to suspect that they eventually relaxed their competitive stances and struck a rapport.

Conclusion

As we have emphasized over and over again in this book, organization life is intrinsically competititive and political. Although few people explicitly recognize the presence of competitive and political forces, or can identify them specifically, we have concluded that most people are implicitly competent in coping with them and in making a response that protects their needs for context. The problem is that most of the responses people make are tactical and that one tactical response begets another.

Breaking this tactical chain requires strategic orientations. People need *perspectives* on the nature of the dominant reality, and *skills* in recognizing discrepancies between this reality and the context needs of specific individuals. People need *perspectives* for recognizing when events hold the potential to be symbolic, and *skills* in comprehending the meaning these symbolic events hold for specific individuals. People need *perspectives* on their own special strengths and needs for context, and *skills* in putting these strengths and needs in focus for others. And people need *perspectives* that alert them to the particular outcomes others need from organization events, and *skills* for making a response that adequately engages and responds to those needs.

How does an individual internalize the perspectives and skills required to assume the strategic orientation? We intend the concepts presented so far to be useful in putting both the situation and the challenge in focus. We expect that the models presented in the chapters ahead, when combined with one's daily experience, will produce the skills required to put this perspective into practice. Our hope is that people will apply the radical management perspective, risk trying out the skills suggested by it, practice them, and learn from their risks and practice. Right now people are doing battle with competitive and political forces they barely comprehend. The radical management perspective will not stop the battle but it should make it possible for people to slow it down and, through their participation, make it less lethal for themselves and others.

SECTION III

What Must Be Known Before One Can Operate Differently

THE LAST SECTION, "Transacting with the Dominant Realty," presented the basic elements of our "radical" perspective. It described how internal politics are every bit as important as rational factors in determining the way events get portrayed. Central to this perspective is what we called "the standard challenge" that underlies each individual's participation: the ever present need to modify the dominant reality to provide more context for one's personal and organizational pursuits. We also described how some people, such as so-called founders, have their subjective interests well embedded within the dominant reality, and derive a great deal of context and power from the current organizational structure. For them the "standard challenge" is to protect against modifications that might disturb their organizationally powerful alignments.

The two chapters in this section complete the framework for our radical perspective. Chapter 10 presents a model for comprehending what specific individuals are attempting to accomplish in their organizational relationships and why they relate to organization events in the unique way they do. Chapter 11 presents a model for how people who work side by side, but experience the same events differently, can get into less personally competitive communications with one another. Thus far we have talked extensively about the subjective component and the organizational dynamics that result from its expression. In this section we use that understanding as background in comprehending what is necessary for people to form collaborative relationships with those who are inwardly programmed to interpret the same work events differently.

CHAPTER 10

Alignment

Fundamental to our model for comprehending what specific individuals are attempting to accomplish in their organizational relationships is the recognition that one can never be sure of what someone else is doing merely by observing that person's outward behavior. Making sense of another person's behavior also necessitates comprehending that person's *intent*. Each individual attempts to realize something unique and personal from the way he or she relates to a job, and learning what that is—the inner needs and themes that generate the observable behavior—is essential to viewing organization events realistically. Without including this component, the mind-set one brings to organization events creates major problems in communication.

Over the years we have witnessed countless instances of people being misunderstood by those who work most closely with them. We have seen numerous instances of people missing each other with the simplest of communications because they were viewing the same events with different internal frameworks and didn't realize it. We have seen numerous instances of people undervaluing one another because, from their frame of reference, the matter was quite straightforward and they just couldn't conceive of a plausible reason why the other person might think differently or perform the way he or she did. In instances such as these emotions run high. People become frustrated and defensive and begin to fight. And because most people lack a model for understanding why the other person is so committed to seeing events differently, and because self-esteem and jobs are on the line, the fighting can be intense. During these times people are inclined to focus on one another's flaws and treat them as if they are core defects. And in moments of desperation they give the consultant a call.

For a graphic illustration of managers with different frames of reference missing each other, and an explanation of why they do, consider the following incident:

Stan, the operations vice-president, was known as a hands-on manager who in a single walkthrough could spot most of a plant's major problems and on-the-fly offer constructive suggestions for fixing them. His plant visits were likened to a physician making rounds, and Tony, the manager of the Seattle plant, was in trouble because he was not picking up fast enough on what Stan was recording on his plant's "patient chart." With his frustrations high Stan called for consultant help. "I need to get Tony back on track" was the verbalized message, but deep down it was much more. Later on Stan admitted, "I was looking for justification for letting Tony go. Let's face it, after twenty-five years with the company that kind of action was going to create a big stir." The consultant did question Stan's intentions, but at the time Stan was not up to being candid. Stan didn't want to give the impression that calling in a consultant was merely a public relations ploy to allow him to say, "I did everything possible to save Tony."

The consultant scheduled a two-day visit to Tony's plant. Stan and his district manager flew in for the opening statement of problems and were scheduled to return the next day for a full exchange of views. The session began with Stan tactfully listing his complaints. He said, "We want to help you, Tony, and we've asked Charlie [the consultant] to make sure we are communicating and to give you a hand." Then Stan and his district manager proceeded to lay out Tony's problems, something they felt they had done many times before. Tony resisted their accusations but when he would try to interrupt, the consultant would say, "Let it go, Tony, tomorrow's dedicated to putting your version on the table."

Stan was clear, to the point, and cited examples. The boiled-down version was similar to one that is often heard.

Stan said, "About eighteen months ago we experienced a problem in Tony's area. There was a drop in profit, trouble with the union, and we were losing confidence. To give Tony a hand we decided to bring in the crew. We brought in the Mc-Donald boys, Joe Saboda, and a couple of others, and for a while Tony did a good job of running what they set straight. Then the operation started floundering again. Tony said he needed to develop his own program for training and merely wanted help in clarifying procedures and obtaining training aids. He only wanted direction on demand. He wanted complete autonomy, with our staff remaining in the background. We did that. We backed off and the plant went down again. I said we've got to do something with Tony because this is one of our most important operations. Now it's slipping again and I don't see the program that's going to turn the operation around. Tony, you say you don't want our help, but I don't see what you are doing. You react after the fact and your reactions are not fast enough." The district manager gratuitously threw in, "Tony, I think you're running scared," and went on to detail why he thought so. On his way out Stan pulled the consultant aside and added, "Don't let Tony fool you; he's a politician. He tries to give me what I want to hear. The trouble is that he tries to satisfy me and not the business."

When Stan and the district manager had left, the consultant turned to Tony and said, "They're telling a different story from the one you gave me on the phone. Where do you think they got their impressions?" Tony answered, "It's a question of timing. Stan is all hands-on and wants what he finds wrong today fixed yesterday. I'm a different type of manager. I rely a lot on people and some things are a matter of time. I don't have Stan's ability to see what's wrong; I have to talk to people and see how things look through their eyes." The consultant said, "I accept that. Do you mind if I talk to your people and see firsthand how the world looks to them? In fact, I want you to sit in with me."

One at a time the consultant interviewed Tony's key personnel. After each discussion he asked Tony what he had learned and then added his impressions. The consultant took pains to define himself as a helper and coach, not Stan's man out to shape up Tony. Nevertheless, the consultant was tough with Tony. For instance, when the sales manager left, the consultant challenged, "You don't really think he's got the proper fix on lost volume?!'' When Tony said ''No'' and detailed precisely what was missing, the consultant commented, ''That sounds right to me, so how many more months do you plan to go before you tell him that?''

After several revealing interviews and frank conversations, Tony got emotional and said, ''I think I'm getting it. I haven't been hearing what people have actually been saying to me. I've been hearing what I wanted to hear.'' The consultant paused sympathetically, and then said, ''It may be that you have a bit of 'salesman's disease.' You talk and sell when there's much more to learn by asking pointed questions and listening. There's nothing wrong with working through people, but you have to develop the skills to face up to what they are telling you and discover how they actually view things. Then, regardless of the delegation, it's your job to set them straight.'' Tony reflected, ''You're absolutely right. I'm dependent on people and I have been taking what they say at face value and not confronting them with how their efforts fail to square with the overall plan. I've made a mistake letting people get away with too much, and then when Stan's group comes in they get overwhelmed with all the loose ends. His style and mine are combining to produce a disaster.''

The consultant agreed and, based on Tony's realization, asked him what words he would have for the office manager who was scheduled to be interviewed next. Twenty minutes into that interview, Tony interrupted and told the office manager that this time he was hearing her words and getting the meaning and that he knew at least three things they could change today to alleviate her problems with the plant. She was stunned by Tony's responsiveness, and when she regained her composure the two of them struck some quick agreements.

At the end of a long and emotional day, the consultant and Tony reviewed what Tony was putting together and agreed that Tony would spend the first part of the next morning preparing his thoughts for Stan's return. Tony felt he had learned a great deal and decided to organize his response as a recitation of what he learned, the problems he now saw, and the actions and programs that might turn his situation around.

Making his presentation, Tony looked like a new man. He held himself erect, sounded strong and confident of what he was saying, and had tangible plans for getting his plant under control. About halfway into his presentation, having just mentioned some personnel shifts that he felt were necessary, Stan turned red in the face and lost his composure. ''Why you sonofabitch,'' Stan interrupted, ''You mean to sit there and tell me back what I've been telling you for the last two years! You've got your nerve.'' To this Tony angrily responded, ''Perhaps you're right, except all I ever heard was how I ought to be running the plant your way—which I could never do. You made me feel like a dummy. When Charlie talked to my people, I heard what I could never accept before but this time in terms I could do something about.''

With a little coaching Tony became strong. He began to see how Stan's special abilities were well tailored to how Stan defined his role and to realize that to be effective, he would have to do things differently. The consultant also attempted to counsel Stan to learn how to manage Tony, given that Tony operates differently than he does. However, this is something that Stan will never accept. Nevertheless Tony is much more successful now and, because of this, Stan doesn't feel the need to intervene so often.

This case illustrates how two people with different personal skills and somewhat different organizational responsibilities would do the same job differently. Tony lacked the skills to do it Stan's way and Stan would never have the patience to do it Tony's way. It also illustrates how each was poised to view the other's mode of operating as one that was ineffective because it presented problems for him and how each needed to structure the situation so that it produced results in the very best way he could produce them. Stan's way was to make himself the hub of expertise and direction and to structure the plant to capitalize on his resourcefulness. Tony's way was to work through people.

Tony's situation illustrates how the flaws in one's style are easily read as basic inadequacies by those who would do things differently, to the point that Stan saw Tony's flaws as constituting grounds for dismissal. This is understandable, because as long as the evaluator, in this case Stan, stays in his own context, he lacks the framework for understanding specifically what the other—Tony—needs to improve. In organizations people who produce the desired results usually survive and can even prosper when deviating from what the boss expects. But most people go through periods where they require coaching and assistance in producing what's desired and expected. At such times they are extremely vulnerable to critique by someone using a different frame of reference—particularly a boss—who wants to use the occasion of the deficient result to push that individual into a framework that's more compatible with the one he or she uses.

We are now at the point where we can talk more specifically about the interests that underlie how someone decides to do his or her job and the needs for context that result. This is a topic that we have studied at length and have written about extensively. In fact it's now been over ten years since we coined the term *alignment* to characterize the unique and personal orientation an individual uses in approaching his or her everyday activities at work.

We came up with the term *alignment* while trying to describe what an individual goes through in attempting to relate his or her subjective and self-centered interests to what he or she perceives as the objective requirements of the job. We sought a way of depicting the balance an individual strikes between his or her self-interested and self-beneficial pursuits and the desire to make a tangible and valuable contribution to the organization. Alignment, then, became our term for characterizing the unique way an individual attempts to line up, *align*, his or her needs for personal meaning, identity, and success with what he or she believes the organization needs to receive from someone in his or her role or position.

There are two major components to the work orientation we are calling alignment: one is personal and the other organizational. In practice neither is 100 percent divorced from the other, for much of what one pursues self-beneficially is associated with what that person needs to do to make an organizational contribution and to become a success; much of what one pursues organizationally is related to one's self-pride and desire to benefit personally from what he or she contributes.

The Personal Component

In many organization settings self-interests are associated with acts of selfishness, evoking a moralistic response even though everyone privately acknowledges their importance and omnipresence. Too often they are associated with blatant rip-offs such as the costly expense account dinner where no business is discussed, the business trip planned to coincide with a family celebration, a favor done with the expectation that it will be returned, and so on. But in the total scheme of things, we find that the blatantly corrupt acts have a diversionary effect that prevents individuals from focusing on the central role self-interests play in determining the orientations people use at work and their reactions to almost every situation.

More precisely, the self-interests that play a role in almost every situation are those of performing one's job using those skills that make an individual particularly effective, the self-interests involved in avoiding tasks that the individual does not perceive him- or herself skilled to perform, the self-interests involved in doing one's job in a way that makes it personally interesting, the self-interests of incorporating those personal and social values that the individual finds essential to his or her self-esteem, the self-interests involved in instituting a job logic that reflects the way one is most comfortable thinking, and the self-interests involved in fitting one's job in with the rest of one's personal commitments.

Our study of the personal and self-interested side of alignment has revealed that people differ predictably in the ways they see events, attempt to structure reality, and in their desires for context. They differ markedly on the above-mentioned dimensions and these differences significantly affect the way an individual decides to perform his or her job. For example:

Skills	• Those who work well through others, such as Tony, do their jobs differently than those who are technically proficient, such as Stan.
	• People with strong verbal skills do more talking and less writing than those who aren't as good verbally but who are excellent writers.
Nonskills	• People who become tongue-tied during conflict avoid adversarial positions, generally appear to get along better, and may at times concede an argument rather than risk a conflict.
	• Introverts and people who don't read others very accurately find ways to avoid groups and team problem-solving.
	• Some people don't feel comfortable selling and they don't.

Interests
- People who like to travel spend more time on the road than people in the same jobs who don't.
- People who like computers and mechanical gismos find ways to mechanize their work and spend more time in the computer room.
- "People-oriented" managers spend their discretionary time counseling subordinates and participating in management discussions where the merits of personnel and the best composition for a particular department are discussed.

Values
- Personal values determine the latitude people extend to those who fall into minority categories (a category may be a viewpoint or a social or ethnic grouping).
- Personal values have a great deal to do with the specific reforms on which an individual decides to take a stand.
- People who value team play take more care in dealing with requests to help another department.

Personal commitments
- Professionals and managers who are single and unattached often pour more energy into their jobs, since they depend on them more for their identity.
- People who are financially secure often scare less easily and don't respond to job threats and intimidation.
- People with young children, sick parents, or a troubled spouse manage their work so as to free up time for family responsibilities.

The Organizational Component

We have found that most people attempt to structure their jobs so that they can give the organization what they believe it needs from someone who occupies their position, and so that they can contribute with excellence. However, what an individual believes the organization needs may be different from what his or her superiors believe, or what is stipulated in the organization blueprint. In fact, sometimes the way one thinks his or her job should be performed conflicts directly with how bosses, peers, and even subordinates believe it should be performed; then one has a dilemma.

Such dilemmas lead to decisions about how one is going to conduct one's affairs, including: holding out and fighting for what one believes is right; capitulating on or sacrificing aspects that one feels are important in favor of aspects valued by others; deciding to make a double effort to include both actions that please key others and actions that conform to one's own beliefs about what the organization needs from someone in his or her role and position. Of course the extent to which an individual perceives a discrepancy between doing what he or she believes is correct and doing what key others see as necessary will determine the extent to which the person experiences him- or herself in a political situation.

Overall Alignment

Alignment is a tricky concept because it presumes an ever-present interaction between the personal and organizational components—between what the individual does for him- or herself and what the individual does for the organization. Thus, if the organization's interests are x and the individual's are y, we claim that every action an individual takes has a xy factor in which the x and the y are inextricably woven together and cannot be separated. People who do not understand the existence of such an interaction are inclined to err in assessing the intent and impact of other people's behavior. Not understanding that an xy factor exists leads an individual to see others either as overly selfish and individualistic in their performance of organization duties, all y, or overly objective and organizationally directed in what they propose as a course of action, all x.

For the most part alignments are enduring, and shifts are gradual and not easily recognized. Changes are observable only when something dramatic occurs in one's life or one's job. Everyone knows someone whose work orientation changed observably when he or she acquired a new skill, received a university degree, went through a divorce, received an unfair review, had a heart attack or a bout with alcoholism; everyone has seen work orientations shift with a promotion, a change of employers, or an assignment for which one lacked sufficient skills or self-confidence.

Personal considerations are all-important in determining how an individual decides to do his or her job. That is, before one's alignment is set, an individual must integrate a great many considerations to create an orientation that will accomplish most of what he or she desires while avoiding compromises that are too personally costly. There are periods in the assumption of every new job and each significant new assignment in which an individual attempts to get his or her bearings and develop an orientation that maximizes what he or she brings to, and gets from, the job. Of course, others in the organization instinctively sense when an individual is in the process of formulating a job orientation. They attempt to affect that person's view of the job in ways that result in orientations that are compatible with their own viewpoints and actions.

After an alignment is formed, it can be likened to a lens through which an individual sees and interprets all organization events. It's an orientation that affects every perception and gives an individual a way of constructing and interpreting situations so that personally meaningful and self-beneficial opportunities are immediately recognizable. There is not enough time to run down a mental checklist of personal and organizational concerns each time an individual encounters a new situation. Alignments give an individual a frame of reference for instantly recognizing the opportunities and threats inherent in each situation and the importance or dismissability of various interpersonal relationships.

Are people conscious of their alignments? Can they tell you what theirs are? Generally, people are not conscious of their alignments and have a difficult time specifying what their alignments are. However, we have found that alignments are not unconscious either; we'd call them preconscious. While few people can state what their alignments are, most can discuss their work orientation so as to reveal where they are coming from and where they are trying to go. They can disclose facts—about themselves and their attitudes towards the job and what they believe is crucial to their company's interests—that will clarify why they arrived at the particular orientation they did. For instance, an individual who discloses that she was raised by overly intellectual teacher parents who pushed her academically effects, in the minds of most listeners, a tolerance and appreciation for the highly intellectual manner she utilizes in addressing problems at work. Likewise, finding out that an individual spent two years managing a foreign sales office that because of its isolation lacked good communications with the parent company can explain a great deal. One develops perspective on that person's independence and apparent comfort with uncertainty and doesn't take personally oversights that result in that individual's lack of communication.

In summary then:

- An alignment represents an internal structure for putting one's every action into personally meaningful terms. It explains how individuals orient to organization events and what they are trying to accomplish both personally and organizationally. In short, the term alignment is a way of understanding an individual's personal relationship with the job.

- An alignment is a maximization, not total optimization. It involves compromises and concessions that an individual has reasoned him- or herself into making.

- An alignment provides a natural way of relating to organization events, making it unnecessary for people to run a mental "computerized scan" for each situation in order to assess the opportunities it offers to pursue what is personally and organizationally important to them.

- Once established, alignments tend to be enduring and subject only to minor adjustments unless a dramatic change in circumstances occurs.

- Alignments can change substantially with major shifts in self-interests and new job considerations. However, change is usually preceded by a period of disorientation and confusion, a period we liken to structure shock. That is, during transitions an individual lacks an integrated way of responding to new organizational events and appears ill at ease and personally awkward.

We believe that there are three kinds of alignments: effective, ineffective, and organizationally successful. We call an alignment *effective* when an individual works out a synergistic relationship between doing what that person needs accomplished for personal reasons and what he or she believes the organization needs and expects from someone in his or her current role and position. We call an alignment *ineffective* when either the self-interests of the individual or the needs of the organization come too much at the expense of the other. We don't see any winners in either of these latter situations; that's why we call them ineffective. An individual who gives too much to the organization eventually begins to substitute organizational satisfactions for self-satisfactions and loses the ability to deviate from the expected. The organization in turn loses the benefit of his or her spark and creativity. An individual who overexploits the organization for his or her own self-interested ends usually suffers a loss of self-esteem and becomes cynical about the institution.

We call an individual's alignment *organizationally successful* when it elicits organizational context. That is, whether an alignment is effective or ineffective, an alignment is organizationally successful when others understand and publicly acknowledge the value of the individual using it. And as we have already explained, such understanding and valuing depends on the presence of three context-setting conditions. First, others must judge one's function to be an important contributor to the organization's mission. Second, others must see one's role as a plausible and effective way of pursuing that function. And third, others must see the connection between one's daily activities and the role and function one has staked out for oneself.

As we have mentioned, people's alignments can change. And when they do, the images that explain these people and their functions and roles to others must be revised. Failure to provide an updated set of images that others can use in judging one's effectiveness can result in expectations that no longer correspond to what one is doing. For instance, some years ago we witnessed the alignment transformation of a twenty-nine-year-old executive, a financial wizard who had risen to the post of corporate controller in a large multinational firm. This transformation took place in a leadership laboratory which was actually a week-long sensitivity training program for executives. When it was over, this executive needed a new corporate image. Examine with us what took place and the need that was created.

At the initial session, this executive bragged about his ice-cold reputation and ability to make tough-minded decisions without compromising his company's profits, particularly by getting rid of people who were no longer competent performers. As the program progressed, he began to develop meaningful connections with several of the grey-haired fathers in the group. This prompted him to tell a story of his being adopted by a well-to-do family who gave him no physical affection and who sent him off to boarding school as soon as he was old enough to leave home. With questioning, he told of his wife's complaints that he worked too hard, was not emotionally expressive, and did not spend enough time with the children.

The disclosure of his personal story evoked a great deal of support from the "fatherly" types, and their response inspired a set of major insights. By the end of the week this man had been transformed into one of the warmest appearing persons you'd ever want to meet. He embraced others, listened solicitously to their feelings, and openly gave emotional responses of his own. Perhaps the pendulum overswung a bit but this seemed understandable to everyone. We felt that with a little help from his wife and his friends at home he would eventually find a happy medium. But what about those people at home? Without a little warning they would think we'd created a monster. And what about those people at work who had built their alignments thinking that they worked for one of the toughest lions around? How would they react to the pussycat they were receiving in exchange?

This executive's alignment had shifted. Accordingly, he needed to establish a new set of images that would create the context for his actions to appear understandable. He needed some coaching to help him produce the road map that would allow others to appreciate his change in attitude and to revise their expectations. He needed a story that would help others to reorient to him, and we feared that his telling it straight would make him too vulnerable. Can you imagine how the emotional thugs with whom he had been associating would treat a story of massive personal transformation stemming from sensitivity training? And who is not suspicious of a personal conversion story?

With these concerns in mind the group suggested he tell a story that, with our input, embodied the elements of context described in Chapter 4. The story concerned his seeing the need for the company to implement some of the modern leadership practices that were introduced at the seminar he attended. His story incorporated the following elements:

- *Function.* As controller, his auditing function extends to measuring real performance, organizational units and people, and not just to monitoring the categories that precedent dictates as having value. His function includes discovering new categories that relate to the specifics of a division's business and to the particular people involved.

- *Role.* His job is to get to know people, to enter into give-and-take discussions with them in order to develop a sensitivity to what they are doing and to what they believe has real value. His role is not merely to monitor the categories that people know are being used to score their performance, but to discover the categories that people believe represent their actual contributions.

- *Activities.* He needs to spend a lot more time with people. He needs to hold informal discussions, attend seminars, participate in any event in which people will take him through the numbers and then tell him the real meaning of their activities.

Conclusion

Some ineffective alignments are organizationally successful; some effective alignments are not. Success has to do with external acceptance for one's alignment, while effectiveness has to do with the personal meaning and self-esteem that come from doing a job that the individual believes the organization needs from someone in his or her position at this particular time. Our books *The Organization Trap* (Basic Books, 1974) and *The Invisible War* (Wiley, 1980) describe the problems created by people with "ineffective" alignments who want to succeed. The former describes what happens to people who have been conditioned to give to the organization at the expense of doing what's personally important; the latter describes what happens to the organization when people think first and foremost about themselves. But, in our minds, the only desirable situation is to have people with personally effective alignments within an organization that is capable of valuing them. When this is not the case, we'd say there's a bad fit.

Perhaps the primary value a construct like alignment provides is causing people to think about the compatibility between their needs for personal context and the reality that is mainstream or dominant in their organization. Without a construct like alignment, people are judged inadequate or incompetent, or are blamed for being destructive when their work fails to measure up to someone else's expectations—perhaps the expectations of the dominant organizational reality. With alignment, one begins to examine the fit between what one is working towards, and what the dominant reality expects. Instances of poor fit can be recognized as such and interpersonal conflict and ego-attacking judgments can be greatly reduced. The biggest toll organizations take from people comes from implying that an individual is lacking competence, personally and professionally, when the way he or she thinks a job ought to be done, or is able to do it, fails to measure up to organizational givens. Alignment is a concept that allows an individual to consider the fit between his or her orientation and the dominant thrust of the organization and recognize when a mismatch (rather than a personal inadequacy) occurs. Like the concept "no-fault divorce," alignment does much to support feelings of self-esteem during periods of vulnerability—those times when people are likely to become defensive, and are inclined to place excessive blame on the organization or, alternatively, to criticize themselves severely.

Sometimes the analysis of a mismatch discloses compatibilities of purpose and orientation and inadequate performance. Here is where the real opportunities to benefit from the concept of alignment occur. Acknowledging compatibility of purpose and orientation allows the potential critic to get on the side of the poor performer, ratifying his or her goals and thinking about how his or her performance can be improved. Over years of management consulting we have found few situations where personal defensiveness did not diminish once it became clear that the individual and the organization wanted the same results and had compatible orientations. In such instances, the *critics* became less punitive and harsh with their comments and focused more constructively on opportunities to coach and on skill improvement. The critics' tone changed because they were no longer battling to assert that the directions they personally preferred were correct. The performers also became less defensive because their basic identities were being recognized—that is, they found themselves being urged to perform more competently in a direction they wanted to take, using skills they wanted to improve. Removing the threat of being judged inadequate, on grounds that were never relevant to an individual's orientation and goals, creates the opportunity for constructive feedback and coaching.

CHAPTER 11

Strategic Realities

Alignment is our construct for describing the distinctive way people orient to work events and the personal goals that underlie the orientation they choose. It represents the unique synthesis an individual achieves in maximizing self and organizational interests. An individual's alignment determines what that person requires in the way of organizational context—how that person needs work events structured and interpreted so that the connection between what that person is doing and what is required is established in a viewer's mind. Of course, different alignments produce different needs for context. Hence, there exists the ever present possibility of conflict between people who are "programmed" to structure work events and interpret the dominant reality differently.

This chapter presents our response to the problems caused by people with different alignments who work side by side attempting to interpret and modify the dominant reality in ways that compete with one another. It examines the options an individual has when the context he or she seeks fails to match up with the needs of his or her associates, and whether or not it is possible for people with good intentions but competing needs for context to transact without conflict. And, it presents our model for how people with different alignments who are programmed to see the same organizational event quite differently can establish trusting relationships with one another.

Tactical Options

As a means of examining the options people have when dealing with those who view events differently, return with us to the episode described at the beginning of Chapter 3. It involved an experienced executive named Chuck who, as a recent hire, was attending his first meeting of an existing management team. To most people Chuck had three options for how he might react at any given moment. First, he could *buy in*. He could listen to what people said, comprehend the version of reality underlying what they were saying, and, where he decided that it was close enough to his own perceptions not to cost him much in the way of diminished personal power and independence, go along with it. To some extent this is what Chuck did but had he proceeded only this way he would not have been able to forcefully present what was unique and important in his point of view.

Second, Chuck could *hold out*. At any point in the discussion he could take exception, saying something like "That's not the way I see it," and then go on to tell "it" like he thought it really was. Of course this second option is not an easy one to choose because attempts to change a group's or an organization's reality usually evoke frontal resistance, sometimes a heated fight. Perhaps the first time Chuck took exception someone would merely say, "Chuck, let me explain our reasoning to you," as if it were Chuck's newness, and not his deficient perspective, that caused him to see things differently. The next time the resistance would probably become more aggressive, depending of course on the seriousness of the issue with which Chuck was taking exception, and the style and open-mindedness of the person whose alignment and needs for context led him or her to defend the status quo. As Chuck continued to take exception, the confrontation would no doubt become more fierce, with group members finding ways to attack Chuck's perspective directly.

Recall that Chuck was a pretty smart guy whom his buddy called a "master politician." Thus Chuck probably realized that he needed to find the proper rhythm between taking exception, in order to get the organization to change its reality to include more of his views and interests, and buying in. There are just so many times that someone can object to a group's or an organization's reality before he or she becomes looked upon as an outsider who doesn't fit in. This is as true for top executives like Chuck as it is for people lower down in the hierarchy. In fact, the corporate world is full of recently hired presidents who are struggling because they are unable to strike a balance between holding out for changes in the existing reality and supporting it.

Chuck's third option was to *play along*. By nodding his head he could give the impression that he was in tacit agreement with what was being said, and the version of reality implied by it, when in fact he thought otherwise. By playing along he could think as he liked and act as he saw fit knowing that he would face little or no direct opposition as long as others were unaware of his differences with them. Playing along with the group's reality would protect Chuck's credibility. In organizations, people like to pick their spots, and you'll recall that Chuck was seen as someone who did such an excellent job of picking his spots that his new buddy saw him as dominating the group.

We've identified three options: buying in, holding out, and playing along. Each of them is *tactical*. They are tactical because their use achieves organizational power for Chuck at the expense of either suppressing his views or antagonizing others—both with costs to the effectiveness of the overall system. But is there an alternative? Is there a fourth option, one that is more *strategic*? What else could Chuck or anyone in a comparable position do when walking into an existing organization with the need to establish a strong role for himself but without sufficient information about the nature, scope, and breadth of the dominant reality that group members support, about the power of that reality and the circumstances for which it was created, and about what others have to gain by perpetuating it? Of course, group members were tactical too. They attempted to get Chuck to go along with their dominant reality without being very explicit about the functions and purposes served by that reality and without revealing their vested interests in maintaining it.

Despite smiling faces and effusive expressions of good will at the time, neither Chuck's nor the group's actions produced much trust. They didn't because each sought personal context at the expense of context for the other. There is nothing unusual about this situation. It is typical of what almost every newcomer faces in an organization, and it is what almost every group's members encounter when transacting with a newcomer or with someone from outside of his or her immediate department or organizational domain. Groups try to socialize newcomers to fit within existing agreements about the nature of the dominant reality, and newcomers like Chuck, who feel their strength and independence depend on resisting such forces, wind up with three options, seldom more.

The Strategic Alternative

Given how most people are used to thinking about organization events, asking for a fourth option is a trick question. But we have been pushing another way of viewing organization events, based on the following premises:

1. People have unique alignments that lead them to see mutually experienced events differently.

2. Organizations create their own ''dominant'' realities, which are born in the agreements that people strike about what way of seeing things is compatible with enough of the interests of enough of the people involved.

3. The absence of explicit disagreement should not be interpreted as people seeing a situation the same way but, for reasons relating to personal interests and political motives, as people willing to allow existing definitions to stand.

A fourth strategic option entails an orientation that is attentive to the context needs of each person. It's an option that requires people to proceed with the above mentioned premises in mind. It demands that people who participate in discussions of organization events be aware that others see situations differently than they seem them. Most important, it requires a commitment to finding a way of defining the organization's reality that acknowledges each individual's needs for a unique context. Of course, searching for a definition of reality that provides enough context for each person and actually coming up with one are two different issues. But when two individuals or, as in this instance, an individual and a group are able to find it, trust and real teamwork result.

When an organization has a way of defining events that provides a good measure of personal context for each member, then people's needs to compete internally, and to vie with one another using political means, subside. We call the achievement of a reality that satisfies the context needs of two or more organization members a *strategic reality*. The word "strategic" is used to express the merging of several different realities into a composite, unified reality that has properties over and above its constituent parts. This reality is likened to what takes place when founders, such as the group we fictionalized in Chapter 7, meet to establish an organization. People create a definition of reality, a synthetic person-made one, that engenders commitment and identification from each person involved. But unlike the founder's reality, a "strategic" reality represents an accommodation. It is born from the pragmatic need to find a way of viewing events that allows people with divergent agendas to cooperate.

Left to their own devices people see organization events in relation to their own alignments and accompanying needs for context. But when people add an accurate depiction of the needs and interests of others to their view of organizational events, and assume the goal of cooperation, then their views change. No longer are they looking merely to satisfy only their own objectives. And no longer do they view an accommodation to the needs of others as merely a social or political necessity. Now their view is stretched to include a way of representing organizational events that allows both them and their colleagues to accomplish their essential organizational business.

Chuck's fourth option, then, was to seek out a strategic reality—a reality that was responsive to the context needs of others and not just his own. In proposing this option we are not suggesting it is something that Chuck or any other newcomer has the power to accomplish unilaterally. In fact, for Chuck to have sought a strategic reality, both his and the management team's consciousness would have needed to be quite different. Group members would be committed to searching for a way of restructuring the organization's reality so that Chuck, or any newcomer, would have a chance of fitting in, and Chuck would be interested in appreciating the basis of the dominant reality and the reasons for the agreements implied by it. Each person would, more or less, recognize the following:

1. My view of reality is based on the particular alignment that I have worked out to make the most of my job. What I see is inextricably tied to the uniquely personal orientation I use.

2. The same is true for others. That is, for me to understand another person's view of an organizational situation, and why he or she chooses a particular course of action, I must also understand what that situation means to that person, where he or she is coming from, and where he or she wants to go. Only then can I begin to comprehend what the organization faces in trying to get quality results from this person, and where this person needs me to modify my organizational views to provide him or her sufficient context to make use of his or her strengths.

3. My job and my effectiveness depend on taking action, not just sitting around contemplating what the situation looks like through the eyes of each of the other people who have a stake in what I do. There are times to act and when I do I will pursue the most effective course I know, which may or may not include accommodations to others.

4. After taking action, I must be careful to avoid communicating the impression that I think that those who would do otherwise are wrong, inadequate in their perspective, or self-indulgent. I must respect the different inclinations of others, recognizing that there are many ways to get a job done, and, while I picked what appears to be the right way, there are other decisions and other ways that are better suited to the needs of someone else.

5. Likewise when others take actions that fail to compute with me, I will attempt to control my immediate frustration and first seek out the framework that motivated their behavior. Then I will decide whether or not that was an organizationally viable way to proceed, what the consequences of proceeding that way are, and what type of response I want to make.

Had group members assumed such an enlightened, strategic view, Chuck's mode of operating might have been quite different. Instead of picking the spots for asserting himself and selectively exposing others to his viewpoints and critiques of their actions, he might have felt sufficiently trustful to make his entire perspective known. He would have provided others with background material for appreciating what he concluded, why he did so, and what he hoped to accomplish. In response, others might have used this information to support Chuck and help him create an essential and meaningful role for himself. In turn, Chuck might have sought out perspectives on key aspects of the dominant reality, what they accomplished for each of the others, how these aspects were arrived at, and then considered this information in the actions he took. In response, the group might have used Chuck's review to identify and revise agreements that were forged under conditions that no longer are present.

If all of this sounds idealistic to you, we agree. The likelihood of finding a group of top managers who, while under fire, are willing to reevaluate hard fought agreements about the nature of their organization's reality every time they add a member is highly improbable. However, we *do* think that management should be aware of the problematic nature of imposing old agreements on newer generations and should periodically review key dimensions of the dominant reality to examine their fit with the alignment needs of those who are currently present. In the next chapter on team-building we'll describe how such a process can be promoted. Moreover, two people can readily create a strategic reality on their own, and oftentimes quite spontaneously, once they find sufficient incentive to face up to the difficulties imposed on them by their different views of reality. People who need to get along, who want to collaborate, can develop the means. The skills are not particularly difficult, but the inner motivation must be sincere.

There's nothing mysterious about the skills for forming strategic realities. They follow directly from the perspective we expound. People need to comprehend the basis of the other person's reality and include it in their consciousness. It's not necessary that they join it; what's necessary is that they accept its existence as a fact and commit themselves to searching for a personal perspective that extends "proper" context to the other. This prevents people from getting caught up in organization politics and duplicitously saying what they feel they have to say about the nature of the dominant reality in order to succeed. Let us illustrate with an example.

After a short "honeymoon" period at work, Herb and Bruce started to clash. It wasn't that serious at first, but after two years their ups and downs were having a cumulative effect. Herb was the corporate executive in charge of finance who had hired Bruce to be the finance vice-president in one of his company's larger divisions. Bruce's job included responsibilities for the accounting department, for administration, and, most importantly, he served as financial analyst and advisor to the division president who, on the organization chart, was Bruce's immediate boss.

Over time, Herb clashed with Bruce on many issues. The first involved reconciling an error-ridden bank statement which Herb felt Bruce had not attended to with the speed its urgency required; the next was a delay in the replacing of the division's controller, whom Herb had closed the book on long before Bruce finally acted; another was over Herb's contention that Bruce should have taken a tougher stand when advising the division president on questionable operating practices that made the company liable to law suits; and still another was Herb's criticism that Bruce did not assert himself sufficiently in establishing the independence of audit personnel.

Bruce had his list as well. Most of them, however, could be subsumed under the heading of not getting enough recognition from Herb. No amount of effort produced a situation that Herb was willing to label a good job, a successful performance, or even substantial improvement.

For a long time Bruce viewed his difficulties as a problem in styles: his was low-keyed and Herb's was hard-hitting. In Bruce's mind, Herb needed things done with the same hard-hitting style he (Herb) would use, and Bruce felt his personal integrity depended on resisting him. In response Herb spent hours trying to convince Bruce that his complaints lay not with Bruce's low-keyed style but with substantive issues—Bruce's low sense of urgency, misguided priorities, and lack of aggressiveness in getting division management to upgrade their financial controls. Bruce listened and listened and complained and complained but could never succeed in turning Herb around. So he concentrated his energies where he could succeed, pleasing his line-boss on the organization chart, the division president.

In a final effort to put an end to Herb's complaints, Bruce asked for a three-way meeting with Herb and his division president. As it turned out, the meeting was an exercise in self-confusion for Bruce. Bruce should have understood that there was no way Herb could assert in front of the division president that functionally *he* was Bruce's boss and that *he*, and not the division president, was best stationed to direct Bruce's activities and assess his performance. Herb was simply not interested in an unproductive power struggle with the president. Three times in the meeting Herb pretended that he was *not* Bruce's boss and that he was willing to go along with the division president's assessment and deployment of Bruce's energies. Of course when the meeting was over Herb was able to explain that he had not "quite" conceded so much, even though Bruce and the president both received that impression. Herb had found himself in a pinch and, as a consequence, had sliced the truth so finely that on another day he could reassert himself without having his words in this meeting thrown back in his face. All capable managers have this ability and, when in a bind, are not reluctant to use it.

Eventually we were asked to help resolve this conflict. While the issues were knotted and complex, by using our model the solution was relatively easy. We used our position as organizational neutrals to summarize Herb's reality for Bruce, and Bruce's for Herb, and brought them face to face so that each could tell the other what he believed and why he felt that way. In doing this we sought to create a strategic reality in which both Bruce and Herb would expand their individual perspectives to include the situation the other actually saw himself in. Up to this point they had been competing, each trying to assert his reality with sufficient force to bring the other around. We sought to dissolve that competition by stating each of their orientations and putting it in context for the other. We gave each the perspective that linked the other person's reality to his organizational situation and skills. We told no one anything that we did not tell the other.

We told Bruce that Herb saw himself as the corporate person assigned to supplement a division with a president who was sales and marketing oriented and who did not exercise sufficient fiscal control. We told him that Herb's apparent preoccupation with divisional problems was his way of finding small issues that could be used to illustrate the bigger lessons. Yes, Herb was preoccupied with the negatives and yes, he was upset with the way Bruce operated because he felt that Bruce, with his low-keyed way of proceeding, was systematically missing opportunities that could educate people up and down the line. Herb wanted leadership, not staff work, and he wanted someone who, by asserting a strong viewpoint, would manage the division president's fiscal response.

We told Herb that Bruce saw himself in a political bind. He was fearful that being seen as a messenger for corporate concerns would make him an outcast on the divisional management team and limit his ability to gain division management's cooperation. We told him that Bruce prided himself on being an individual who could juggle many balls at once and who sought change by steadily moving items towards completion, not by creating conflict. We also mentioned Bruce's frustration in never getting credit for the undramatic things that went right, and in being abused each time something went wrong.

We told them both that, contrary to the image he was projecting, Bruce understood that Herb was his "real" boss and only had resorted to politically strengthening his allegiances to the divisional team once he figured out that he was in a no-win situation with Herb. We told them both that Herb was using a hierarchy of priorities for viewing accounting and financial activities and that he had a problem with Bruce devoting substantial energy to an activity on the upper end of that hierarchy while something more basic was problematic and unresolved. And, we were able to explicate the criteria Herb seemed to use in ranking Bruce's activities on that hierarchy.

As a result of our explanation, a strategic reality was formed. Each now tells a story that is more respectful of the other person's needs for context and the role that person needs him to play in supporting it. Within corporate circles, Herb publicly ackowledges that he squeezed Bruce too hard and that it is essential that corporate executives support Bruce's position on the divisional team. He says, "We'd better respect his dilemmas or his managers will cut him off. Then we'll have no way of knowing where our problems are until they blow up on us." Privately Herb says, "We put Bruce in a tough spot. Expecting a junior guy to walk the thin line between corporate and division like that is too much to ask. We forced him to seek refuge in a partisan divisional role."

On the other hand, Bruce is much clearer about the role he has to play. He has finally comprehended Herb's priorities and agrees that he must push the division to build a stronger foundation for itself. Within the division he publicly acknowledges his responsibility to push corporate concerns but always in the context of his division team membership. For instance, he says, "We've got to act fast on this before the guys upstairs in corporate get wind of it and come barging in with some half-assed solution that doesn't work for us." Alternatively, he says, "My corporate boss has convinced me this is one of those issues that we in the divisions can't allow to slide." And he now grasps that his main job is to fix the system that produces fiscal improprieties and not just to set specific matters straight.

Both Herb's and Bruce's relationships to the "problem" have shifted. Formerly, each was looking to make a response that was positive for the organization and good for himself; now their accounts have been mutually modified in directions that also display sensitivity to the other's situation. Herb is genuinely supportive of Bruce's need to be a member in good standing on the divisional team, to manage with an even-tempered tone, and to have his contributions valued. Likewise, Bruce acknowledges that Herb is correct in attempting to reform divisional fiscal practices, and understands more clearly how corporate has been attempting to manage around a division president whose focus they find lacking.

After two-plus years of not getting along, Herb and Bruce have made real progress in working together. Today they function with a greater understanding and appreciation for the role the other is attempting to play and what they must do to support it. And while some significant differences exist between them yet, they do a much better job of working them through. The story they tell gives more significance to Bruce's role on the divisional team, to Herb's role in advising him, and to both of their responsibilities for advocating divisional practices that attend to corporate concerns. They now possess the type of shared reality we call "strategic." They each understand the other's needs for context and, while they are not governed by what the other needs, they find easy ways to take the other's concerns into consideration and, more importantly, they find respectful ways to negotiate their differences at moments when no middle ground seems to exist.

Are there organizational costs associated with people expanding their view of reality to take active account of another person's situation, thereby diminishing the strength of their positions in the adversarial process? No doubt there are. In our experience the slogan "There's no such thing as a free lunch" seems perfectly suited to life in the organizational world. However, what's most apparent in this situation are the gains. The efficiency of Herb's and Bruce's communication has improved dramatically. No longer does every difference produce the contentious exchange that leads them each to go home and beat the dog. Actually neither has a dog but Herb has been known to eat too much and carry an unhealthy amount of weight, and Bruce has mean streaks of sending barbed memos that insensitively taunt another department about its organizational flaws. Both of them are much happier now and Herb's weight and Bruce's memo writing show it. Moreover, Bruce has the job affirmation that he needed and lacked and Herb has established the control that will improve his candidacy for a bigger job.

We hope readers see the importance of the reality-bridging process. People can easily form strategic realities on their own once they make the mental shift and acknowledge that the other person, by definition, comes to an organization with a unique set of interests which lead him or her to see organization events in a unique way. This set of interests must be articulated or at least tacitly understood before one can work harmoniously with that person. This attitude is the bulwark of expanding one's view of organization events and forming strategic realities with those with whom one closely works, with whom the slightest difference can create a charged situation and ignite a political response.

Strategic realities do not require reciprocity, although reciprocity is desirable because it usually leads to trusting relationships. However, one person can discover much about the reality of others who have not yet become interested in his or her reality. And expanding one's perspective to include concerns for the context needs of someone else does not mean becoming a captive of that person's needs. It simply gives one the added consciousness that makes planning and formulating a successful course of action more realistic. And such consideration, when recognized by another, will usually engender a desire to match the sensitivity of the individual who initiated it.

Up to this point we have emphasized only the benefits. However, by no means are strategic realities only positives for the organization. In their zeal to get beyond an adversarial or conflict situation, individuals or groups sometimes strike agreements and make operating assumptions that prove invalid for other groups who are affected by how people in their unit or organization think. A strategic reality may turn out to be little more than a "pact" about how organizational events are to be viewed, in which the motives of two or more individuals are advanced at the expense of others in the corporation, at the expense of greater organization effectiveness, at the expense of consumers' interests, at the expense of stockholders having their investment appreciate, at the expense of government agents enforcing mandated regulations, or you name it.

Sometimes people in adversarial positions possess a greater need for a strategic reality than their resources or perspective will allow them to achieve at the time. The result can be a reality that is materially invalid for most of those agreeing to it, and its presence only adds to the schisms between the realities that these people live privately and the dominant realities they use in expressing themselves publicly in the organization. For example, we know of a dispute between a female boss who didn't want to add to her reputation of being "tough on men" and a male subordinate who wanted to make peace with her and keep his job. Quickly the two of them managed to cover up their difficulties by deciding that the cause of their conflict could "more appropriately" be blamed on the people in operations and that procedures for auditing their work needed to be enforced more stringently. So they mutually agreed to blame operations while privately they continued to keep an anxious eye on each other.

To us the test of a strategic reality is the extent to which it both strengthens and empowers the people who formulate it and strengthens the organization systems affected by it. For example, two people can't just get together, decide that each is doing a great job, and vote one another a pay increase that compromises their credibility with others. What's more, the validity of a strategic reality depends on how well it considers the realities held by outsiders and the needs of the organization to maintain a competitive position in each of the market domains in which it operates. For example, at the height of a severe recession with national unemployment at 11 percent the management of the Atari Corporation publicly announced with no apology or explanation that they were eliminating 1700 jobs and moving their production operation to Hong Kong. To us it appeared that their timing and matter-of-fact attitude set off many negative reactions which we'd guess ultimately hurt them in the marketplace. No doubt the strategic reality that produced this decision was well debated within the firm, but the decision—or at least the way it was announced—cost the firm considerably.

Over time, as people and situations change, strategic realities become institutionalized and operate as *dominant* realities. Some of these strategic realities retain their power and validity for long periods of time. They serve as essential orientations to people inside the company as well as to outside constituencies. Companies like IBM and Procter & Gamble have well-articulated and distinctive dominant realities that orient just about everyone who comes in contact with their operations. For instance, consumers know Procter & Gamble is committed to high quality, government regulators know it is committed to ethical and valid presentations of consumer safety data, advertising agencies know that their promotions must be wholesome and not tarnish the clean-cut image the company seeks to present, and so on.

On the other hand, some companies have done a poor job of transforming strategic realities into dominant realities that communicate a distinctive identity. For instance, our students report that there's not much to choose between when considering a position with one of the Big 8 public accounting firms, or a movie production company, or an aerospace engineering firm. Whether one works for Northrup or Rockwell International, for MGM or 20th Century Fox, or for Peat Marwick Mitchell or Arthur Young seems on the surface to make little difference. The unique identities of these firms are eclipsed by the image of their industry as a whole. And in our minds these organizations pay a substantial price in employee self-esteem and loyalty by lacking the strategic realities that would lead the corporation to a more distinctive identity.

SECTION IV

Operating Differently

THIS IS our "applications" section. It applies the radical management perspective to the kingpin categories of organization effectiveness—teamwork, leadership, motivation, and power. How managers position themselves with respect to these critical areas is all-important in determining the conditions that enable people to be seen in the proper context and develop trusting relationships. Alternatively, managers can operate in ways that force people to seek context and acceptance for their subjective interests by using the covert processes associated with organization politics.

Unfortunately each of these categories—teamwork, leadership, motivation, and power—is already fraught with politics. This results from people relying on overly rationalistic mind-sets that direct them either to exclude the subjective element or to place excessive controls on its expression. In contrast, our radical perspective directs people to seek ways of addressing management issues with the subjective element aboveboard, treated as a variable to be consciously considered and dealt with explicitly as an essential part of the problem-solving process. This does not necessitate highly emotional meetings where people are encouraged to discharge pent-up feelings, although occasionally such airings are appropriate. It entails simply comprehending the alignments that underlie the behavior of the people with whom one works, and formulating organization plans with the subjective element more realistically considered.

The way we see it, the rationalistic mind-set leads directly to a tactical response. It puts people in power-laden situations where they and others are competing for different interpretations of the organization's reality without revealing the central force behind their advocacy—their own subjective interests. It subjects people to a cross fire of scenarios until the subjective element becomes so absurd and obvious that an incentive is created for people to recast their advocacies in less self-serving ways. And all the while each participant's tactical objective is to create a logic that overwhelms that which is being proposed by others.

In contrast, the goal of radical management is not to overwhelm other people or to suppress their divergent interests. It is to create a better fit between two or more self-interested advocacies that momentarily are perceived to be competitive. The radical mind-set proceeds on the assumption that each organizational response is codetermined by personal considerations, and that the only accurate way to transact with someone is to relate to the framework that actually underlies that person's advocacy. That is, only after the interests that determine the directions of another individual's organizational commitments are known and made part of one's organizational dialogue with that person can two individuals develop a "strategic" context—one that puts each on the side of the other's personal and organizational effectiveness, searching for a mutually compatible and organizationally productive response. Each of the "applications" chapters that follow builds upon this radical management perspective.

CHAPTER 12

Team-Building

With a founder's reality, an organization can be expected to function with nearly perfect teamwork. Then reality is an amalgam of people's needs, interests, and overlapping perceptions of the marketplace, and everyone knows what is expected of him or her and, with minor exceptions, can be counted on to meet these expectations to a tee. However, with time and the influx of new personnel, important aspects of the founder's reality are displaced. They are displaced by implicitly struck agreements that, taken in total, constitute what we have termed the dominant reality. But the roots of this dominant reality are located in compromise and politically negotiated agreements, and it lacks the personal commitment that people give to the founder's reality. Thus, with the dominant reality, perfect teamwork is far from a given.

In theory, a dominant reality provides the same information, goals, objectives, ways of operating, etc., that formerly were provided by the founder's reality. However there is far less overlap between it and what people need and believe actually exists. People with different alignments privately experience and interpret the same events differently. And while publicly they acknowledge and support what they understand constitutes the agreed-upon dominant reality, privately they remain ever alert for opportunities to modify it. Of course, people with different alignments push for different modifications and over time they begin to clash. At first their clashes are tacit and result in frustration and tension. Later their clashes are explicit and manifested in public debate and controversies in organizational direction.

Eventually such clashes take a very political and overly personal form, with people openly blaming one another for what went wrong. And while insults over misguided motivation and inadequate skills fly back and forth, our radical management perspective indicates that fundamentally this is not what is wrong. What's wrong is structural, not personal. Too many differences exist between the orientations of the people who are supposed to be integrating their work efforts and functioning as a team and that which is sanctioned by the dominant reality. What is needed is a revised picture of reality, one that recaptures degrees of overlap that the organization possessed when composed only of founders.

The radical management framework points the way. It posits strategic reality as the goal. It directs people to revamp the conflict-ridden dominant reality in ways that maximize individual, unit, and organizational strength and compatibility. Promoting teamwork, then, entails promoting processes that create a better synthesis of effort among people who constitute the organization. Teamwork means revising key dimensions of the dominant reality to fit better with the alignment needs of individual members while maintaining active concern for the needs of external constituencies and the marketplace. In essence, *the goal is to upgrade the dominant reality and make it a strategic one.*

A great deal of the time we have spent promoting teamwork has been in consulting activities that our clients call "team-building." While the format for our work differs depending on the particular individuals and situations involved, our intentions are always the same. We seek to get people with overlapping responsibilities to hold the conversations that make their work together more effective, more efficient, and more enjoyable. And we seek to establish these qualities at both an individual and an organizational level. Thus, while our explicit focus is on enhancing organization effectiveness, we are also diligent in our concern that such effectiveness not take place at a cost of significant personal sacrifice or exploitation of others. In fact we're constantly looking for opportunities to show people how to use work problems as vehicles for learning how to deal more directly with the subjective element. We actively promote the educational dimension of people's work together to the point that privately we don't differentiate between our consulting on team problems and management development.

We began our team-building work many years ago. From the start, we have believed in an "equifinality" of effort, thinking that there are any number of ways for a group of people to work together and achieve their goals, and feeling that, all things being equal, people should choose the route that is most personally satisfying and meaningful for them. At the core of our early work were the technologies of group dynamics that promote candor, feedback, understanding, respect, and ultimately trust. We structured situations so that people could speak candidly without permanently hurting one another's feelings. We wanted people to listen carefully to what others had to say, learn from the feedback, and have these experiences in a setting that promoted mutual understanding and respect for each individual and his or her uniqueness.

Our effectiveness in promoting teamwork increased considerably when we finally recognized the inherently political dimension of all organization work—that which is produced by people manipulating reality to create the contexts that allow them to succeed. This led us to articulate the construct of *alignment* to explain why people position themselves the particular way they do. And when we conceived of the solution that people need to build strategic realities, our work in promoting teamwork took a significant step forward. A contrast of the more traditional approach to team-building, which we used for many years, and the approach that makes individual alignments explicit provides a useful means of illustrating the power of our enhanced understanding. Incidentally, the adaptations we've now made are also applicable to pairs of individuals developing two-person trusting relationships on their own.

Team-Building Prior to Alignment Theory

As we said, there is no standard format for our work, but prior to our articulation of "alignment" we might have responded to a request to promote teamwork in the following way. We would begin by talking with the boss and getting his or her picture of the group

situation. We would listen to his or her spontaneous story and ask
a series of questions aimed at seeing what work issues he or she
thought the group needed to address, what might be the desirable
outcomes, and what he or she felt each of the other members
ought to do to make a more effective contribution, going down the
list of names one by one. Typically we concluded by asking the
boss what he or she wanted to be doing five and ten years out.
This question was prompted by our desire to comprehend the personal direction behind the boss's strivings.

Equipped with a reading of the boss's perspective and orientation, we would get permission to interview each of the other
group members and when we did we would ask a parallel set of
questions. We asked:

1. What needs to happen for this organization (the team or
   unit of immediate concern) to operate more effectively?

2. What needs to happen for the boss (insert his or her name)
   to operate more effectively?

3. What do you need to do to operate more effectively yourself?

4. What does _____ (the name of each person on the team)
   need to do to operate more effectively?

5. What role can you play in helping each person to do so?

We began each interview by telling the person that we were
not the boss's man out to get him or her to shape up and that we
endeavored to represent each person's interests along with the
needs of the group. Proceeding this way seldom produced more
than a moment's reluctance to be candid. People seemed to enjoy
telling their work story to someone whom they perceived to be a
neutral; afterwards we'd ask whether anything was told to us that
should not be repeated. Only occasionally did people ask for confidentiality and many of these requests were withdrawn once we
made it clear that we did not intend to be messengers who con-
veyed information that was more appropriately delivered in person. Rather our intent was to attend a meeting, chaired by the
boss, and to act as facilitators in helping group members hold the
discussion that might improve their team's effectiveness.

Given that our interviews disclosed that all group members
possessed a certain minimum amount of good will for one an-

other, and that they had a sincere desire to collaborate, we would recommend that the boss convene a two-and-a-half to three-day meeting to discuss the issues people raised in our interviews with them. We usually requested that the meeting be held away from organization premises so as to avoid interruptions and to get away from the physical cues that lock people into established ways of relating to one another.

The typical meeting began with an introduction and statement of objectives by the boss followed by a period of data-sharing by us. Using long sheets of newsprint, and taking care to preserve anonymity, we presented our lists of what we heard group members say were the important personal, interpersonal and team effectiveness issues that needed to be addressed. Included were lists of what each individual, including the boss, needed to face in order to make a more effective contribution and a list of effectiveness issues for the group as a whole.

While our work with each group was different, the overarching patterns were similar. First there was exposure to the lists we prepared and questions for clarification. Next, group members attempted to deal with personal effectiveness issues and to set straight those who may have "misperceived" them. This process was usually enlightening, both for the person who was the target of the critical feedback and for those who stepped forward to deal with him or her. Usually we would direct the group first to engage issues concerning the boss, in the belief that the boss's constructive candor and responsiveness would set the climate for candid exchange among peers. To protect against the possibility of a boss getting too defensive and possibly traumatizing the group with his or her reactions, we would, prior to the meeting, brief the boss on those tough issues we could foresee.

With a group of five to eight this second stage productively lasted well into the second day. It was a stage in which group conflict, personal clashes, and defensiveness had to be overcome before people could begin to engage each other in a more respectful and influential manner. The potential for lasting enmity was minimized by the fact that everyone's effectiveness was scrutinized and discussed, and by the presence of a facilitator experienced in managing this type of process.

The third stage began when the group switched to dealing with the issues that people had listed as problems in their work unit's effectiveness. Here the group directed its energy to issues of improving internal systems and work processes and addressed difficulties in producing what external constituencies expected. Usually residuals of the personal feedback stage affected this discussion, for group members occasionally lapsed into periods of holding one another responsible for problems in their unit's effectiveness. Nevertheless, the personal and interpersonal work performed prior to reaching this stage eventually cleared the way for collaborative strategies and agreements. And almost without exception, group members experienced a greater degree of cohesiveness, mutual respect, and team commitment by the end of the two to three days. Most important, they developed group-level strategies for dealing with their unit's major problems.

Over the years we found that this approach offers an efficient method for reenergizing flagging groups and is a relatively low-risk method for getting individuals who are not working well together back on track to solve group-level problems. However, too often only the symptoms are treated. While this remedy is highly effective in getting a group past its current impasse, it does not give group members a deep enough understanding of the origins of their interpersonal conflicts to prevent their recurrence. Seldom did we find significant gains lasting more than eight or nine months. Then the group required another event, usually somewhat different in design, to address lingering issues and to deal with new frictions. And of course each time we worked with a group, the composition was somewhat different and new members needed to become familiarized with and be included in agreements that had been concluded prior to their coming on board.

Team-Building Using Alignment Theory

Our concept of team-building matured considerably once we started working with alignment theory. To begin with, our definition of team-building expanded to include any experience that familiarizes people who work together with the assumptions and premises that underlie a cohort's orientation. As consultants we try to utilize any situation which:

1. Establishes that people who are working together have unique alignments, and can divulge specifically what their alignments are

2. Familiarizes people with key dimensions of what their cohorts need in the way of organizational context

3. Creates a forum for modifying a group's dominant reality in ways that are more consistent with the needs of group members

To promote this perspective we look for any situation of interpersonal controversy, conflict, or difference in expectation that seems to matter materially to one or more of a work team's participants. We ask some variation of the following questions: "What could be causing a highly competent, well-intentioned individual to function the way this person is functioning?" "How is this person attempting to be competent?" "What is this individual personally trying to achieve?"

We have also modified the way we conduct offsite team-building sessions like the one we just described. Prior to these sessions we conduct ourselves more or less as we always have, making sure to establish a relationship with each team member and to solicit his or her perspective on what the others and the team face in becoming more effective. The major difference is in the way we begin a meeting.

After the boss's statement of objectives we now give a brief presentation on alignment and then hand out a set of questions which we call a "Personal Orientation Questionnaire," asking team members to spend forty minutes to an hour thinking about their answers and jotting down notes to cue their memories later on. The questions we hand out are chosen for their ability to elicit information that informs others about their alignments if that individual is willing to tell others what he or she thinks. A sample of the questions we include is given here:

PERSONAL ORIENTATION QUESTIONS

First, describe a bum rap or overly simplistic category others have used in describing you and either tell why you are different now or why their statement was simplistic or too categorical.

Then answer the following:

Personal

1. What are you trying to prove to *yourself*? State specifically why.

2. What are you trying to prove to *others*? Give an instance that illustrates how you have sought to demonstrate it.
3. What is distinctive, maybe idiosyncratic, in your manner and way
of seeing the world? State why this way of being is important to
you.
4. What style of life are you trying to maintain or achieve? Does this
entail a change in income? geography? family size? (etc.)
5. What statement do you want to make with your life? Why?
6. Who are the people who have played important roles in your life?
Describe what those roles have been and the parts of them that
you consciously try to emulate.
7. What motto would you like to have carved on your tombstone and
how do you want to be remembered by the people who are close
to you?

Career

1. What profession do you want to wind up in? (If you are an engineer and you say "management," tell why. If your target profession is different from your current one, say how you plan to get
into it.)
2. How did you or will you develop competency in that profession?
3. What do you want to accomplish in that profession?
4. What honor or monument would you like to have symbolize your
success in that profession? Explain why it would constitute a personal hallmark.

Organizational

1. What has been your image in your organization and what would
you like it to be?
2. What's the last important lesson that you learned? Explain either
what you had to overcome in learning it or why you weren't able
to learn it sooner.
3. What is the next lesson you need to learn and what are your plans
for doing so?
4. What would you like to be doing two to five years from now?*
5. What would you like to be doing ten years from now?*

Job

1. What's your job function? What are the basic operations you perform, what activities are necessary, what are the necessary skills,
and which are the important relationships?

*Think of "doing" in terms of a specific assignment (job, position, status) and
specify it in terms of a specific role (player, coach, expert).

2. What job aspect would you like to have disappear? Tell why you find it unproductive and/or unrewarding.
3. Describe a recent work assignment that gave you a personal feeling of challenge and exhilaration. After describing this, state what you think were the unique dimensions or characteristics of this situation and why they were such a turn-on for you.
4. State the strengths you bring to your job and describe the self-aspects that are your greatest resources for learning and developing new strengths.
5. Do not state weaknesses, but do state the important specific lessons that have recently (last two years or so) made it possible for you to perform more effectively at work.

After a period of reflection we ask group members to take turns answering their list of questions aloud for the others in the room to hear. We caution people not to divulge anything they do not want known by those who are present. We ask the group for a pact of confidentiality, saying that the specifics of what is talked about today are only for those who are present in the room. And we tell those who are listening to limit their questions to points of clarification about what is said and not to debate what are now being divulged as facts about the other people. We should add that we don't suggest this exercise if our experience in individual interviews indicates that someone is not likely to deal maturely and discreetly with what others might disclose.

We're constantly amazed by how much personal material people decide to reveal. We tell people it's fine with us if someone decides not to say very much and caution them not to succumb to group pressures to conform. But people seem to welcome the opportunity to explain the basis of their orientation, particularly after someone else's story has increased their own understanding and empathy for that person's position. Consistently, people reveal much more than the situation we've constructed seems to demand. And typically, those who provide the deepest revelations gain the most in the way of group understanding and appreciation.

We're always impressed by the significance of what people learn by listening to someone else's report and the respect shown for the vulnerabilities that are disclosed. And most fascinating of all is to see the source of the trust that is created. While a substantial amount of trust is generated when people learn the substance of what someone is actually up to when he or she behaves the way he or she does, a significant amount of trust is also created because the disclosure makes people feel vulnerable, and the disclosers tend to feel good about people who now better understand the basis of their orientation and treat their foibles and flaws with respect. It should be added that most of what is learned is implicit because disclosers seldom talk about work specifics and listeners normally don't say very much although their facial expressions and body postures often communicate a great deal.

The personal orientation discussions run about half to three-quarters of a day and by mid to late afternoon the group is usually ready to receive the list of concerns developed from our interviews. The difference in response between how a group that has had a personal orientation session and one that has not is dramatic. People now transact with increased understanding for one another's alignments. This causes them to put the other person's actions in a context that is more compatible with what that person is up to, to appreciate the inevitability of personal expressions and idiosyncratic ways of operating, and to develop more understanding for what an individual is attempting to achieve by the unique way he or she has chosen to proceed. Here is an example.

In response to the question that asks an individual to describe a *bum rap* in how he or she is seen by others, a talented program manager named Mitch matter-of-factly described the unfair way subordinates and some peers were inclined to characterize him as "uncompromising" by pointing to a number of situations in which superiors found him a very easy and cooperative person with whom to work. Of course, during our interviews we had heard many criticisms of Mitch—how he insisted that others work within his structure and made little effort to extend himself to theirs. Our newsprint feedback contained several comments in which we had attempted to articulate this perception tactfully.

Later on, when describing the people who had played important roles in his life, Mitch talked about his father, and when he did, the bum-rap mystery instantly cleared up. Mitch told how his father had engaged with Mitch in only those activities that he himself enjoyed and avoided those that didn't personally interest him. Almost instantly it became clear that Mitch had internalized this mode of operating; he felt it was his "right" to demand that those at his level and lower down work within his preferred structure, and likewise it was his duty to accede to the preferences of those higher up. Later, when it was time to discuss the list of issues concerning Mitch's effectiveness, the conversation went very fast. Someone said, "From what Mitch said before, I can easily understand these comments." Mitch said sheepishly, "I do too, and, what's more, now that I think of it I act the same way with my twelve-year-old son." The group felt no need to dwell on the feedback items; they understood that Mitch would work on this and do what he could to change. They no longer saw him as the "enemy." Now they could get on Mitch's side, empathizing at moments when he was stuck in a mode where his behavior was frustrating to subordinates; the ground was broken for helpful advice from his peers.

Preceding the feedback with a sharing of personal orientation answers speeds the group's process, all but does away with conflict and clashes, and adds considerable validity to the problem-solving discussions. People who have more understanding of one another's alignments are much more practical in their dealings with one another. Going through the personal feedback items becomes an exercise in rapport-building as people spontaneously change from a critical posture to one of insight and affirmation. When people see the connection between how an individual operates and what is established in his or her character and makeup, they become as supportive as they were morally indignant and critical a few hours before. This does not mean that they accept all of another individual's flaws and specific struggles; it means they get to know *the individual* with his or her flaws and struggles and gain insight into why they exist. They develop perspectives that later can be applied in comprehending the unspoken subjective attachments others have to an issue that they formally advocate on "objective" grounds alone.

The same is true of problem solving. Knowing another's alignment leads people to stop the finger-pointing, blaming, and unrealistic planning. Instead they think about the talents and skills of the people involved, what needs to be done, and what arrangements of people and resources can accomplish it. Instead of insisting that others live up to every specific responsibility of their jobs, as one may feel the right to insist, one learns to make realistic assessments of what it is practical and reasonable to expect from a person with a particular alignment and the corresponding needs for context. Team problem solving involves building on one another's alignments, and when sacrifice is required, each team member has the reference for appreciating each other's contribution. The result is that instances of selflessness and sacrifice are noticed and appreciated with net gains to team morale.

On-Line Team-Building

By no means does all team-building take place in a group and, of course, most occurrences do not require the assistance of a professional consultant. For our purposes, *team-building includes any two-person conversation in which information is exchanged that enhances an individual's understanding of the internal framework behind the other person's behavior.* Certainly it is desirable that these exchanges eventually be comprehensive, or else one or the other of the participants may walk around with an inaccurate view, causing him or her to misinterpret the other. Thus, at some point a formal recap of the discussion is necessary in order to ensure that each person's total picture of the other is comprehensively stated and known.

Holding an "alignment" discussion gives people the insight to better utilize another person's skills. When this happens, it can enhance that person's organizational self-esteem.

Until one of these exchanges, Carole, the managing editor of a national magazine, had always thought of Louise as a good writer but someone she had to defend against criticisms that she was too detail-oriented and slow. Carole's typical response to a criticism of Louise was something like, "I *know* she's too slow but if you treat her with patience, eventually she'll come through for you. Personally I've always been pleased with the quality of her production, even though it takes a while to get." After the two held a discussion in which Louise's alignment was disclosed, Carole developed the perspective to make a far better response. Now when someone complains, Carole says something like, "You're right; Louise is detail-oriented but that's because she sees elements of a situation that escape a lot of eyes. Watch her, question her, ask her the significance of the so-called small issues that seem so important to her. If you hurry her, all those meticulous perceptions become obstacles; if you work with her and give her a little support, she'll write brilliantly for you.'' With that type of support Louise did very well.

Certainly Louise's keen eye will not be relevant to every writing assignment or to the magazine's need to crank an article out fast. However, with the proper context, she'll be deployed differently, and should it be necessary to put her on one of those ''quick and dirty'' assignments, Carole can clarify this up front and state explicitly that this is one assignment where Louise will have to compromise her style. And should so many of these ''quick and dirty'' assignments come along that Louise doesn't get a chance to use her meticulous eye, both she and the magazine will have a way of saying ''poor fit.'' Then, Louise can go some place else with no hard feelings on her part and without putting the magazine through one of those shabby separation processes where everyone else wonders, ''Where is the axe going to fall next?''

Learning about someone's alignment gives people who want to collaborate necessary perspective. It releases them from their inclination to change the other person to better fit with their own needs, and provides the knowledge required to link up with the other person and make use of what he or she does well. This lessens the other person's need to misrepresent him- or herself as being more skilled or differently inclined than he or she actually is. There is a bit of paradox here. Dealing with the *subjective* side of an individual up front does more to maintain the discussion at an *objective* level than holding the discussion on a rational and objective level from the start.

Of course, most people avoid exposing their alignments and engaging in discussions that familiarize others with their personal orientation and subjective needs for context because they fear others might exploit their vulnerabilities and weaknesses. We have seen enough exploitation to certify that such concerns are often real. No doubt this is why most people err on the side of being overly cautious about whom they choose to open themselves to.

What, then, is the best strategy? Withholding disclosure and not giving anyone a solid look at your weak spots is a good personal survival strategy in many situations. But deploying that strategy when it isn't necessary goes a long way towards creating the precise situation that people disdain. Certainly team-building and episodes like the one we described between Carole and Louise can reverse the negative trends in an organization's culture and create an atmosphere of trust, openness, and added productivity—something that can happen only when people are *not* looking over one another's shoulder, thus distracting one another from concentrating fully on the work elements of the job.

Back to our team-building example. We have found that groups who go through the routine that we have outlined, in which group members expose their personal orientations, are easily able to use the rapport they create in their daily dealings back at the "plant." What's more, they achieve a better fit with one another. This is not to say that they don't have conflicts and personality clashes. They do, and like any set of associates they have personal issues and differences in judgment to work through. But the ground has been broken for them to develop more empathy with one another and to act strategically in their dealings. In most cases, the need to overwhelm others tactically and hammer them into submission is abated.

Sharing one's personal orientation coupled with follow-up problem solving becomes a variation of a founder's experience. It gives people the perspective needed to reorient themselves, make small shifts in their alignments, learn where the others stand, and make appropriate modifications in their organization's or their unit's reality. This creates a *strategic* reality that is based on knowledge and respect for individual differences, where enough is explicit between people and their cohorts that one can be direct in expressing differences. People then appreciate the inevitability of the other person's "win-win" orientation and possess the inclination to expand their own to "win-win-win."

A question that's often raised is how large a team can benefit from such an approach? This is a good question, and we have to admit that we've never applied our technology on an institutional scale, nor would we at this time advocate doing so. To us, an organization is a confederation of different units, and it is each leader's job to create teamwork and trust in the unit of his or her responsibility as well as to form linkages with adjacent units. Consultants can help, but leaders have the responsibility. We have a lot to say about this in the next chapter, "Leadership."

A Note of Caution

In fairness to our readers we have to end this otherwise optimistic chapter with a word of caution. The constructs we use and the applications we propose represent a cultural transformation. Most people work in a rationalistic environment that makes very different assumptions about how people should organize to perform work, how they should communicate, and what each can expect from others. Its assumptions are different from the assumptions and premises that underlie what we are proposing and what we, utilizing our expert status, are able to create. In particular, most people work in environments that become very moralistic about the injection of self-interests in the organization. These are environments in which what we called the *xy* factor is not accepted and that discount the appropriateness of all actions in which the self-interested sides of one's motivations show. This leads us to a very specific suggestion. Seek all instances to exchange personal orientations, involve yourselves in discussions that parallel those we create using the personal orientation questions, but don't ever admit to a self-interest in a concrete form. Of course each action will always contain a self-interest component; we hope we have established this. But in today's organization environment there still is too much encultured self-doubt and morality for people to endure hearing others admit to a tangibly selfish act. Give people the information that reveals your alignment, seek insight into theirs, and talk openly about your needs for context and how you and they can create a reality that does the most to establish the conditions for everybody to be valued. But avoid making a concrete statement such as "I'm delaying the Toronto meeting a week because my wife wants me in town during the preparation for her sister's wedding" or any other confession of self-interest. What people need are insights into your frame of reference, not reminders of your self-indulgences.

CHAPTER 13

Leadership

We teach courses in leadership. We teach them to executives, we teach them to management trainees, and we teach them to MBA students. And in each group a single question is raised with such frequency that we think it must be the most commonly asked question in the management classroom. We're asked, "What is the difference between a leader and a manager?" It's a question asked so often that we're lucky it leads directly to lively and informative discussions. It raises issues that we find particularly appropriate, since from our perspective *there exists a major crisis in American management: not enough managers are leading.* In our opinion, it is management's reliance on a tactical orientation that makes it difficult for them to lead. For an example of the leadership void produced by the tactical orientation, observe the management style of an executive named Ben faced with two of his lieutenants fighting.

The fight was the typical one that takes place when a powerful manager loses his patience and goes on a crusade to tighten up controls and someone tries to oppose him. Marty had become that impatient manager and he was wielding a big club. He decided the time had come to crack down and put teeth into management's imperative that people toe the line, stop all the discussion and participative nonsense, and just plain do their jobs the way they are supposed to be done.

Al was Marty's opposition. He too wanted to see results. But unlike Marty, Al was not willing to let his impatience catapult the company into the type of crisis management where disrespect and blaming people are rationalized as the only way to produce results. He agreed that tough times required a more disciplined effort but felt a note of urgency could be interjected without getting brutal. He was aghast watching those who worked directly for Marty knuckle under to Marty's hardline stand, and felt it was his responsibility to dig in and oppose it.

Marty and Al each knew that the other was a threat. They had become daily adversaries. Every issue became an opportunity to assert their divergent orientations and block the other from pushing his. And, increasingly, their dialogue was becoming combative and personal.

The boss, Ben, was the key. He was the target of their daily lobbies. Ben was the open-minded type who thought both Marty and Al were making effective contributions, and confined his comments to saying so and to voicing disapproval towards each of them for not getting along. Ben was working hard to get sales up and production costs down, and in his big picture this conflict between his two key managers was a petty irritant.

Al felt he had done all he could as a peer to educate Marty and finally had given up. He knew no strategy for changing Marty's attitude other than to wait for senior management to get fed up with Marty's hard-line tactics. Privately, he never missed an opportunity to portray the flaws in Marty's thinking to Ben, as well as to higher-ups when they visited. He was careful never to attack Marty directly, but always to make sure that the flaws in Marty's thinking were visible if one cared to notice. Al also felt that higher-ups understood that his stand was based purely on his concern for the good of the company, since as head of industrial relations, he had nowhere higher in the corporation to go.

Marty did have room to progress. He was head of production and there were a number of upper-level spots in the corporation for people with his background. But in his mind this was not the reason for the battle. The problem was the effectiveness of operations, not job politics. The way to get promoted was to succeed at what he was currently doing, and that meant getting people to do things right by restoring discipline and order to the system. In his mind, everyone working for him agreed, and Al was merely being an obstructionist.

As the conflict became more open and punitive, the pressure on Ben to resolve it increased. Finally he went to Al and said, "Marty is wrong and he's got to see that. You are right and it's your job to get through to him. Since you are the people expert I'm counting on you to take the initiative." Al responded with a stunned look of amazement. He had no idea what else he could do.

How did this situation reconcile itself? It was reconciled the way such situations too often get resolved. The tough guy got his way. The deciding moment came when it was least expected. In a private meeting Marty climbed all over Ben on a separate issue that involved Ben's lack of leadership. It was an instance where Ben was clearly remiss and Ben, in order to put out the fire quickly before his corporate management could get wind of the problem, bought Marty off by agreeing to get rid of Al and to assume the disciplined course that Marty had been advocating. There are lots of ways to get rid of people in organizations and there's no need to detail the way Ben chose. Suffice it to say that one day Al was gone and everyone got the impression that the reason for it was Marty.

What's wrong here? Certainly it's not that two managers had strongly competing orientations that they could not resolve on their own. What, in a large organization, could be a more common occurrence than overzealous competition among managers who are entrusted to advocate for different functions and make sure their own units are not neglected or disparaged when someone else pursues his or her cause? Was the problem Ben, and his weak leadership? Yes, the problem was Ben but perhaps not for the reason you think. To us it was not because Ben didn't take a strong stand with Marty and tell him to merge his ideas with those of Al. And, it was not because Ben couldn't help Al to take a smarter course in getting Marty's attention. It was because Ben had an inadequate concept of what he was trying to build and how that was going to be accomplished.

Clearly, Al would not have lost his job and Marty would be a better manager today had Ben possessed the vision to lead. But he lacked a vision and because of this could never really assert himself. Ben was not out front, the direction and the process for getting there were always being subordinated to the immediate high-priority item. People knew they needed to do their jobs well, but they never understood precisely where the company was going: the part of the market they were heading toward, the internal management style they needed to implement, and the organization structure that would carry them ahead. Ben never told Marty and Al what his future plans were, why each was essential to the company, and specifically what role each needed to play in supporting the other's progress.

Ben never made the connections—between what people were doing to be productive today and what the company needed in order to move ahead—solid enough for his managers to see. His appeals for Marty and Al to get along were not based on how they needed one another in order to take today's company to where it should be tomorrow. And in practice, a guy like Ben is not very different from the majority of well-intentioned managers we meet each day. They lack a vision of what they are trying to build, and they lack insight into the organizational processes that will take them there.

Now to the question, "What is the difference between a leader and a manager?" As we see it, the essential difference lies in the degree of involvement in defining a unit's path and direction. Leaders play an important role in defining what the organization needs to achieve specifically and uniquely—the images that determine the orientations people bring to their jobs. Managers work within the images that leaders create and if none are forthcoming they work within the conventional ones prescribed by the American management culture: promoting hard work and team-play, increasing production, cutting unnecessary costs, building morale, and so on. Leaders create reality. Managers work within realities that already exist. Leaders innovate and break from tradition. Managers construct the goals that fit within established frameworks and decide which of the established processes will be used to pursue them.

For Ben to have been a leader he needed a vision of tomorrow that he believed in strongly enough to use as a guide for his everyday actions. He needed a plan, a story, a scenario to which he could point in staking out a direction for people to follow. If he didn't have one, then he should have been out conducting the research needed to create one. And it was not necessary for him to create it alone. All leaders are not visionaries but all leaders have a vision. If you had asked Ben, he would have said he had a plan. All managers do. But if you then had listened to his words, you would have seen that the plan he had was merely that of attending to managerial basics such as getting sales moving in a recessionary economy, or reducing fixed production costs to excise slack when sales are insufficient to support overhead. Ben had not communicated where his division was going and how it would capitalize on its unique strengths in the specific situation in which it found itself. This created a void into which two subordinates with strongly opposing styles could enter and clash.

To our way of thinking, and to that of some leading organization theorists,* a leader needs both a concept for where the organization should be heading and a concept for the organizational processes that will take it there. Of course a leader also needs the ability to put those processes into operation.

A person in a leadership position operates as a manager when he or she lacks one or the other of the above concepts, or both. A person with a concept of what the organization should achieve but an ineffective idea of the organizational processes needed to carry out that concept is not leading, because too many people who are necessary for moving the organization ahead won't know what to do or how to coordinate with others working towards the same end. Conversely, a person who is committed to some process, trusting that involvement in that process will produce a vision of where the organization should head, often gets his or her group lost in day-to-day events. We now recognize that this was the big mistake many managers made in promoting "participation" in their organization. Participation is fine, but only after the direction has been specified in a sufficiently tangible form for people to be sure when others are talking about the same thing and when they are missing one another. One can't expect to lead others when either the vision or the process is unspecified. Leadership requires followers, and in today's skeptical management atmosphere it is terribly difficult for people to follow if they don't know where they are going or how they are going to get there.

*E.g., Warren Bennis, who in his recent book *The Leaders: Strategies for Taking Charge*, (Harper and Row, 1985), mentions several attributes of successful leaders that are relevant to this discussion, such as a compelling vision for where the organization is headed and the ability to state that vision in a form to which others can easily relate.

People in leadership roles often lack the concepts that will move their organization ahead. The reason may be understandable, such as when someone with a new assignment is just getting a sense of the situation, or a recent change in external conditions is just being noticed, or there is a change in key personnel or other resources and the impact is still being assessed. In such situations, a potential leader may go for a period of time merely keeping things on an even keel, waiting for a concept to emerge. But in our experience, the search for missing concepts must be active. True leaders don't relax when their plan is not apparent. They become more energetic than ever in figuring it out. And once one has a concept and focuses on the dimensions one wants people to use in relating to their organizational experiences, it is success in getting people to recognize and observe these dimensions that demonstrates leadership.

Leaders chart the course to which people affix their alignments. Their visions establish the dominant realities to which people are asked to relate in thinking how to maximize their personal needs for meaning. Thus the routes that leaders choose are of high importance in determining the orientations that people assume at work, and have importance above and beyond the leader's ability to enforce what he or she mandates.

Of course, all of the above is contingent on a leader's ability to create the setting for people to build trusting relationships, for without trust the most intelligent organizational directions go unrealized and the most efficient processes are opposed. It is not enough for a leader to specify direction and the processes for getting there; he or she must also take action that builds and develops trust among those whose teamwork is necessary for carrying out that specified direction. Trusting relationships are what allow people to work together productively in moving their organization ahead.

Leadership and Trusting Relationships

Recall that the capacity to form trusting relationships depends first and foremost on context. People trust those who put them in the proper context and distrust those who resist the images they seek to establish and/or whose needs for context compete with their own. And the directions leaders identify, along with the organizational processes they invoke, are crucial in determining the opportunities for people to find context. Directions that deprive people of context by creating a group of outcasts, or a department whose functions are no longer valued, or people who feel disenfranchised, or preferred modes of operating which diminish the value of other modes that people use, produce personal dilemmas in being valued that people are not apt to accept lying down. No one in his or her right mind is about to support a leader who seeks to institute directions that diminish what one stands for, or processes that make it more difficult to get one's point across, without offering a way of being valued that can be used in its place. Yet many in leadership positions make the mistake of supporting one group or one way of operating at another unit's expense. For instance, we know a recently appointed chief executive who is so wrapped up in his pet disciplines of finance and accounting that he turns a deaf ear on projects that are not fully supported by finely tuned analysis. The result is a dramatic reduction in the number of new project submissions from marketing and R&D, historically the sources of money-making ideas for that business. In response their managers resist the chief executive's every proposal on the grounds that "We need to oppose him just to get his attention."

In our book *The Invisible War* (Wiley, 1980) we mentioned three functions leaders are uniquely positioned to perform that facilitate the development of trust. Time and experience have increased our confidence in the validity of these functions, and we are now able to add to and embellish the descriptions we previously offered.

As we see it, leaders can support the building of trusting relationships in at least three ways.

1. They can help people to better understand their own unique needs for context and the opportunities to establish images that get that context valued.

2. They can help people to respect the needs others have for context, and to learn specifically what those needs are.

3. They can help people create a bridge between their needs for context and the needs of others to produce strategic realities that are mutually beneficial.

We call the first trust-building role *counseling*, the second *team-building*, and the third *brokering*. Specifically, here is what's involved.

COUNSELING

There are two goals to counseling. The first is to assist an individual in working out an effective alignment, one that simultaneously attends to personal needs and to the needs of the organization. The second is to assist an individual in achieving context, in finding ways to get others to recognize that the orientation produced by his or her alignment represents an important organizational contribution. Both of these are essential to an individual becoming a *success*, whether success is measured in the mind of the person or in terms of his or her value to the organization. A person who lacks a self-context can never succeed in his or her own mind, and a person who lacks organizational context—an orientation that others understand and value—can never succeed in the workplace.

Counseling begins with the leader's ability to understand and enter the reality lived by the person whom he or she is attempting to assist. It entails starting with as much of a *tabula rasa* as one can discipline him- or herself to have, and asking questions like the ones we mentioned at the end of Chapter 12. It entails understanding the other person's alignment and communicating enough of that understanding to have that person recognize that he or she is understood.

Of course, leaders are not blank screens. They have definite opinions about how specific individuals can contribute and what possibilities exist for that person to take a role that moves the organization ahead. However, it is only after the leader knows what the individual is attempting to achieve personally and self-interestedly that he or she can give intelligent advice about how that person might reorient to organizational events. Leaders must understand that everyone's first obligation is to him- or herself, that people ally themselves with organizations in order to pursue goals for themselves, and that all alignments are born in self-interested pursuits that cannot be ignored. Thus, counseling takes self-interests as a given, and the leader's job is to show people how they might pursue their interests in an organizationally constructive way.

Now, we are not suggesting that people never sacrifice in an organization. Organization life at its essence is a matter of sacrifice, compromise, and external commitment. But we caution the would-be leader who believes that an organization in which people are sacrificing more than they receive in return, or more than their other options require, can achieve stable or long-term success. Counseling must proceed with the assumption that people affiliate with an organization to maximize their personal priorities. If an individual's role cannot be constructed so that he or she can also pursue what is personally and professionally important, then everyone's interests are served by that person going somewhere else. The leader's job is to help people find ways to do more for themselves and more for the organization simultaneously. Here lies the big opportunity for payoff. Questions of motivation disappear when an individual is able to make the connection between his or her organizational assignment and what he or she is pursuing in the way of personal interests and meaning. When these connections are not made, questions of insufficient motivation are ever present in the minds of those who supervise them.

Now we can be clear. The leader must first get into a person's frame of reference before seizing on opportunities to give advice aimed at advancing what the organization needs. He or she then must be cautious not to suggest any way of revising one's orientation that violates that individual's self-priorities. By no means are we advocating that the leader should subordinate the needs of the organization. For instance, recently we sat in with an executive who was interviewing a manager he wanted to hire for an important divisional post which would entail a cross-country move. The executive needed the post filled by the following month, and the candidate wanted to wait another year in order to follow through on his commitment to allow his son to complete the last year in his current high school. Then, when the boy left to go away to college, the family could move. Seeing this as a given, the executive was ready to drop the topic and withdraw his offer when he got the idea to ask, "Is it possible for your son to begin his adjustment to university one year early?" Curious, the candidate asked, "How's that?" The executive explained that he was questioning whether the son might be able to stay behind in the current city with arrangements for him to come home for holidays, as if he were going away to school a year early. Of course, the leader added, the company would view the boy's travel as part of the family's moving expense. This option had not occurred to the recruited manager, and the way it was offered communicated respect for the commitment the manager had made to his son. What's more, the suggestion was such a big hit in the manager's home that it became one of the foundations for a mutually trusting and respectful relationship between the two men that reaped benefits at work.

Throughout this book we have emphasized that working out an effective alignment is one thing, but that having that alignment recognized as organizationally valid is quite another. In fact, at one point we went so far as to state that an effective alignment that is not recognized by others, where an individual lacks context, should not be considered a "successful" one. Who better than a boss or "leader" is there to advise an individual on how to posture his or her alignment to achieve context in the organization? And who besides the boss or "leader" is better stationed to counsel an individual on how to relate his or her personal orientation to organization affairs? Thus, counseling extends to helping individuals relate their private realities to the dominant reality of the organization. A leader understands where the opportunities for forming sharp images lie and can advise people how to engage these opportunities without detracting from the strategically important issue of building trust between them and the people with whom they associate daily. The leader knows the organization givens and understands what might be considered variables open to revision. Social science research has repeatedly demonstrated that marginal members lack the security to deviate from a group's norm, while it is the centrally positioned who feel sufficiently secure to consider what might be revised, modified, and changed.

TEAM-BUILDING

Team-building is the act of helping people put others in context. The goal is to help people see beyond the view of reality produced by their own alignment. The team-builder helps people to put another individual's behavior in the context of what that individual is actually attempting to accomplish. Leaders have unlimited opportunity to play this team-building role, and the particular way they choose to play it is not important. In the last chapter we talked about making team-building a two- or three-day event. Here, we want to discuss the daily opportunities that someone stationed in a leadership position has for team-building and, in particular, the opportunities created when listening to someone describe his or her grievances and criticisms of another teammate. The challenge is to use the occasion of a particular criticism as an opportunity to promote a better understanding of the frame of reference used by the person who is the target of the criticism. Of course it's far easier to help someone else to acquire such perspective than to provide it for oneself. Thus everyone needs someone else's help in putting those who have not performed as one feels he or she was led to expect in their proper context.

How leaders portray one person to another is probably the most important single factor in determining whether or not people lower down in the organization decide to make a personal commitment to the organization and trust one another. Leaders who are respectful in their presentations of one person to another, who respectfully interpret one person's actions to another, do a great deal to promote team cohesiveness. Leaders who assume one frame of reference, theirs, and who do not respectfully inquire into the reasons behind someone's "deviant" performance, establish a climate of parochialism where others feel similarly entitled to criticize those whose actions fail to correspond to their viewpoint. Every information exchange, every project update, and every lunch time conversation offers someone in a leadership position a chance to promote interpersonal tolerance and understanding, and how that person responds in these discussions sets a tone for the entire organization.

Unfortunately, too many managers are far better at "putting down" those who appear to think differently than they are at "putting them up." That is, when faced with someone's deviant position or behavior, their response is more likely to fall within a structure that diminishes that person than one that enhances him or her. We have often said that the test of a supportive boss is whether or not he or she is able and willing to put a subordinate's actions in context when facing someone who has a criticism of that subordinate. In this regard, many managers have such a weak grasp of their subordinates' value that they accept a criticism at face value in order to protect their own credibility and stature.

Yet the really successful leaders operate differently. They miss few opportunities to present critics with the perspective that can help those critics understand why the subordinate functioned as he or she did and to add perspective that makes it easier for the critic to team up with the person whose actions have been frustrating him or her. Of course the tendency to overidentify with the critic is a phenomenon of the wider management culture; adding perspective or defending one's subordinate is seen as defensive, soft, and displaying a lack of hard-nosed, objective thinking.

In our consulting, we frequently ask critical managers "Why do you think someone as capable and as intelligent as this person thought to behave in the stupid manner you just observed?" This is our shorthand way of cuing a manager that the person being criticized is also a quality individual and that a critical perception is an opportunity to learn more about that individual and the orientation that underlies the behavior they witnessed. As we've been emphasizing throughout this book, in an organization no behavior stands on its own. Everything that happens takes place in a special context. And when someone else's behavior does not compute, then it is time to make inquiries in an attempt to find the context in which it does make sense. Criticizing prior to understanding the other person's frame of reference is an indirect power tactic aimed at establishing the dominance of the framework from which one's objections stem and at punishing the other person for not abandoning his or her framework and conforming to what one expects.

Some of the time, of course, the reason behind someone's criticism is an orientation that conflicts with the person he or she is criticizing. Such was the case with Marty and Al in the story mentioned earlier. No amount of interpersonal understanding was going to resolve their disagreement. In such instances, where the alignments underlying a dispute are recognized and understood, it is the leader's job to take a stand and to stop the conflict before it becomes abusive and organizationally disruptive. This is not what Ben, the boss, thought to do and we fault him for this. His weak attempt to resolve the conflict was limited to stating that both Marty and Al were wrong to fight and that they should go out behind the barn and settle it. His inability to assert leadership provoked Marty to make his point of view a crusade and left the organization defenseless with only Al standing in Marty's way. Many people in leadership positions make the mistake of thinking that others can settle disputes over orientations without their taking a stand and playing a role. Thinking this way is a mistake.

Certainly the leader must draw a fine line between intruding too far into the relationships people have with one another and staying too far outside of them. A leader's style will depend in part on his or her personality, and in part on the skills that he or she uses in intervening in organizational matters and the system he or she envisions for people dealing fairly with one another and establishing a climate of trust. Regardless of a leader's specific actions, the important thing is to focus on what one is trying to create and to examine how one's behavior and style contribute to or detract from what each group or team of managers is trying to achieve.

BROKERING

There are two goals to brokering. The first is external: to get one's unit or organization appreciated and valued in the spheres of its wider involvements. The second is internal: to align people within one's unit to achieve a more valid response to what relevant outsiders need and expect of them.

In practice these two goals are reciprocal. Leaders solicit the viewpoints and perspectives of relevant outsiders and encourage those inside their unit or organization to deal responsively with them. Then leaders arrange conversations aimed at familiarizing outsiders with the unique and specific ways their units are attempting to relate with them and, in particular, how their units can be of value. Internally, this means helping people to better comprehend the realities for which they are being asked to manage a response. Externally, it means educating outsiders on how to make optimum use of the products, resources, talents, and capacities that people in their unit possess.

Brokering works by creating strategic realities. It entails leaders creating bridges between people (or groups) with different alignments who, left to their own devices, would seek contexts that place them at odds with one another. It also entails searching for a view of reality that provides context for each while appearing valid to those external interests to which these people (or groups) must also relate. Leaders are constantly involved in discussions where reality is being defined and debated. The organization gains considerably when leaders are able to figure out a new way of framing events, one that bridges the needs and interests of all the involved parties. Certainly this was a function that Ben should have played for Marty and Al, who needed a third perspective that would give context to each of their alignments. In our minds, Ben let his organization down by not conducting an active search for a perspective that empowered both managers.

There is a danger in brokering, and it is one that we introduced in Chapter 6 when we mentioned the problems of using the shared fate approach. It is the problem created when someone in a brokering position constructs a vision of reality to which the people he or she must deal with are not able to relate. A leader must maintain a delicate balance once that leader decides to advance a reality that others are expected to join. A proposal must be presented with enough force to get each of the parties to take it seriously but without so much force that people feel it imposed on them.

By far the most desirable brokering position is one in which the leader creates circumstances that allow those with different and divergent realities to seek a joint perspective on their own. The leader who attempts this should establish some up-front parameters and not face people who have strong and emotional differences with having to figure things out all on their own. In our experience, many leaders instinctively understand this and present antagonists with two or three alternatives and a request that they get together to decide on one. The listing of alternatives exposes participants to the leader's implicit assumptions and establishes the constraints on anyone's private notion that he or she can overwhelm the other and dominate totally. The failure to provide alternatives was another of the mistakes that the boss Ben made with Marty and Al. Had he done so, their dispute might have come out differently, and each could have gained from having to open his mind to the benefits in the approach the other was attempting to advance.

Everything we have said so far depends first on the leader's understanding that reality is mutable, and, second, on the presence of work associates who are committed to finding a way to make their personal contributions organizationally valid. The success of what we are advocating also depends on leaders making sure that their constituencies retain an awareness of the interests of relevant third parties—consumers, stockholders, government regulators, and the like—who take an active interest in how the organization conducts its affairs.

Thus a leader's brokering role includes both the joining of needs for context among members of a work unit or organization, and making sure that insiders are accurately apprised of the needs and thinking of those outsiders whose views are important in deciding the value of what gets produced inside. Brokering, then, centers on a reconnaissance function in which leaders solicit the viewpoints and perspectives of relevant outsiders and seek to get those inside their unit or organization to deal responsively with them. By no means do we intend to imply that those within a work unit become slaves to external perspectives; in fact it is the leader's role to lead the way in deciding which discrepant realities can be dismissed, to set outsiders with mistaken expectations straight, and to advise those who transact with his or her unit or organization as to what set of expectations might get them the most of what they want.

Conclusions

Throughout this chapter we have been careful to speak about leadership functionally, as if jobs at every level of the organization can have a leadership component. What's more, we have been careful not to portray leadership as a function that accrues to all high level jobs. Of course leadership is a quality that depends on the eye of the beholder, and some people automatically attribute this stature to those at the top of the hierarchy without considering the kind of direction they truly provide, how well they establish the conditions for others to follow their direction effectively, or whether or not they help outsiders value what their work units produce. These are matters about which we feel quite strongly. In fact, throughout this discussion we have attempted to discriminate between leaders and managers, the latter being people who are in positions that may or may not afford opportunities to lead and, in any event, have not seized upon the leadership opportunities afforded to them.

Now we can address the second most frequently asked question that we encounter in the management classroom. It is one that directly follows from the first. That question is, "Are leaders born or can they be made out of mortals like us?" Of course people don't actually say "mortals like us" but we usually catch their drift. This is a question on which we vacillate. On one hand, we have seen some natural leaders who never needed to set foot in a management classroom. On the other hand, we are in the business of teaching leadership skills to a spectrum of people with a variety of capacities and we have seen some amazing results. We have also seen some people who have actively sought education, consciously attempting to incorporate every fine point the literature has to offer, but who fall far short of becoming competent leaders.

On balance, we do come out on the side that leadership can be learned by most people and that the majority of professionals and managers have the capacity to become competent and even outstanding leaders. Moreover, we think that the majority of people who already occupy high level managerial positions would do well to work on becoming better leaders. Sometimes the directions that uniquely capitalize on an organization's strengths, resources, and market opportunities will spontaneously occur to someone in a leadership position, and sometimes they will require months of open-ended inquiry and surveys of other people's opinions. Sometimes the slogans that communicate one's ideas will be attained without much trouble and sometimes they will require an arduous process. Some leaders will be lucky enough to inherit an organization or organizational unit where people have context and respect one another and some will have to concentrate on creating the circumstances for people to develop confidence in one another and take the first steps towards trust. And sometimes one will find oneself with the wrong people to perform the required organization job and will have to go through the jarring process of making personnel moves and reconceptualizing what is possible and selling these changes up and down the line to everyone involved.

Leadership takes work. It takes an ability to analyze the nature of the organization's reality and simultaneously to track the extent to which that reality creates conflicts for the individuals who are required to make the organization work effectively. It takes a sensitivity to those third parties who are concerned with the organization's functioning and whose response is key to the organization's credibility and success. And most of all, it takes respect for human beings and the perspective that people have much more at stake in their jobs than just moving through the hierarchy. Most people's jobs are central elements in their identity and what happens at work is a part of the self-concept that accompanies them into every sphere of their life and existence. People who assert leadership on the job can make a large and positive impact on how people see their lives overall.

CHAPTER 14

Motivation

Motivation. What a term! Managers use it all the time and, to the best of our understanding, all it provides is a false sense of security. Usually it's a term applied to others—to change the way someone else orients to a particular situation. And usually it's used in the spirit of figuring out how to get that someone to assume an approach which, given the manager's frame of reference, is out of sync with the high-priority items on that person's mind. Think about it for a moment. What has this frequently used term ever done for you? And what could it have done for the practical real-life situations depicted in this book? For instance:

Could the proper motivation cause Louise, the detail-oriented but brilliant writer, to produce more rapidly?

To us, once you understand what Louise has to offer, speed is beside the point.

Could the proper motivation cause Mitch, the manager who got along well with superiors but not well with subordinates and peers, to assume a more collaborative stance with subordinates?

To us, no real change was possible until Mitch made a connection between how his father treated him and how he treats his subordinates and his own son.

> *Could the proper motivation have helped Stan, the hands-on manager, to propel Tony, the manager who needed to work through people, to address his work situation the way Stan thought he should manage it?*

To us, Tony lacked the skills and aptitudes to manage Stan's way competently.

> *Could the proper motivation have caused Chuck, the executive who joined an existing management group, to take a collaborative, non-ego-centered approach even if the group he was joining did not change its attitude about the dominant reality?*

To us, such action would have come at the expense of Chuck weakening himself in order to fit in, thus denying the organization the best of what he had to offer.

> *Could the proper motivation have caused Ben, the executive with fighting subordinates, to take timely action to resolve that dispute?*

To us, such action depended on specific leadership skills that neither Ben nor his boss were aware that he lacked.

The Tactical Use of the Term Motivation

If the term motivation doesn't apply to situations like these, then where is it used and why is it used so frequently? It is used in situations where one or more supervisors or managers attempt to establish as a given their own reality, or a dominant reality in which they have vested interests, and to *correct* the orientations of those who don't see things their way. This usage obscures the fact that most organizations lack the capacity to confront individual differences and problems of poor fit in a direct and open-minded manner. The orientation behind this way of proceeding is tactical to the point of being ultra-authoritarian unless the person who is the target of the motivational appeal lacks internal focus and is requesting managerial help. We say "ultra" because the questions underlying most uses of the term motivation are of the following quality:

- "How can I get this person to want what, given my internal orientation, *I* want and to function in ways that are compatible with how reality appears to me?"

- "What means are at my disposal to reward and punish this individual so that he or she will have reason to function as I have specified?"

- "How can I enforce agreements that were explicit at another point in time or that are implied in the present job situation, and that my role and responsibilities entitle me to expect from those who report to me, but that, for reasons unknown to me, they don't want to uphold?"

These questions illustrate both the tactical meaning managers typically attach to the term motivation and our radical view of how people need to be treated in order to work in a spirit of teamwork, cooperation, and trust. We find the tactical interpretation a diminishment of the individual and what he or she has a right to expect from a job. We say diminishment because an individual's deviance from practices that make little sense in his or her own internal framework are often labeled "deficient" with such forcefulness that the word "deficient" is generalized beyond one or two specific acts to describe that person's entire usefulness to the organization. "Deficient" is an assessment that can only accurately be made once you understand an individual's skills and aptitudes and the organizational issues and personal themes that orient him or her.

Before we venture much further we need to stop and mention what we do agree with in the way management theorists commonly use the term "motivation." We do believe that there is a standard set of personality issues that concern each person and which should be understood and considered with reference to classes of people and not just one individual at a time. For instance, all people have a need for self-esteem. Thus, we feel each newly proposed organizational practice should be examined from the standpoint of how it affects everyone's desire to be seen, valued, and appreciated for themselves, beyond what they contribute tangibly to the productivity of the organization. There are also other needs, well documented in the literature, such as needs for achievement, personal power, affiliation, and security, with which, we believe, those who manage an organization should also concern themselves. Management should provide the opportunity for people to satisfy all of these needs, on terms that will vary with each individual. However, even when managers know a particular need is universal, they should not assume they know the specific form necessary to satisfy a given individual. Over years of listening to people talk about motivation, we have yet to meet the person who felt good about hearing that his or her superior was about to begin a campaign of motivating him or her, even when the superior claimed to be taking this person's self-esteem and ego needs to heart. In too many situations motivation is a term applied as management's substitute for knowing enough about an individual to understand why his or her actions make sense.

The Strategic Use of the Term Motivation

Now that we've stated what troubles us about how the term motivation is used by managers, we can be more direct in stating our viewpoint. Until one gets a glimpse of the unique orientation that determines the strength and quality of another individual's participation at work, one's ability to comprehend what that person is actually trying to accomplish in his or her organizational actions is severely limited. As we see it, *motivation entails helping another individual mobilize his or her unique strengths in the service of an organizational cause that has purpose and meaning to that individual*. Also, it entails helping another individual relate to issues and projects that represent someone else's concern, and to see how that can be done on terms that are acceptable *to that individual*. It does not mean using one's superior position to dominate an individual and to force a subordination of that person's self-interests to the needs of the organization as one sees those needs existing.

To us motivation does not mean a manipulation of externals for purposes of getting another individual to produce what you want produced in a way that is good for you. It means an inquiry into that person's life and career to understand and appreciate where that person is coming from, where that person is attempting to go, and how that person is hoping specific actions will accumulate to accomplish a major personal goal. The objective is to determine whether or not this is a person you can team up with, and exactly how that teaming up might take place.

To us the term motivation has value as a *question*, not as an answer. As a question one is oriented towards finding out what motivates this person; as an answer, motivation is a term that leads one individual to assert his or her own preferred direction as an organization standard, and to manipulate another individual to reorganize his or her activities to fit that standard. For instance, as an answer we know a manager who thoroughly frustrated her superiors by "successfully" repelling every attempt to motivate her, but the organization kept her on because higher management felt her technical expertise was indispensable. Called in to help, we formulated a motivation *question* and the perspective for accepting her became immediately apparent. It turned out that this manager was the only child of deaf and mute parents, and from age four on, her job was to help her parents transact in the world of words. This created in her a special and somewhat skeptical attitude towards the established way of doing things, along with a reliance only on what made personal sense to her. Once this was known, people were better able to understand the unconventional way she transacted with them and why she took a skeptical view towards all established systems. Immediately, many of the strengths she brought to understanding what customers and outside vendors faced when dealing with the intricacies of her company were utilized to the company's advantage. Perhaps more importantly, she began to see how her unconventional style could be turned into an organizational strength. As a result she has been able to earn two quick promotions.

Skills

Two sets of skills are required of the person who wants to be responsive to the construct of motivation as we are defining it here: helping another individual mobilize his or her unique talents and efforts in the service of an organizational cause that also has meaning to him or her. First, one needs skills in reading another person's view of reality, and sensitivity in understanding the basis of the unique orientation that individual decides to adopt. Second, one needs skills in visualizing how others can relate to projects of mutual concern on terms that are acceptable to them. These skills are of critical importance to the manager who hopes to make him- or herself relevant to another person's motivational scheme.

SKILL 1: READING ANOTHER PERSON'S VIEW OF REALITY

We have already begun the discussion of ways an individual might go about learning the unique and specific facts that have significance in revealing how another person views reality. In presenting our views of alignment and team-building (Chapters 10 and 12) we listed dimensions and questions that can be used in helping one individual see another person's perception of reality and in learning about the orientation that lies behind the specific attitudes and behavior that one observes. The questions we listed are *guides* for inquiry and are not intended as a comprehensive list of what is needed to reveal the orientation of any specific individual or to probe any particular set of circumstances. Moreover, people are complex and in the search to comprehend patterns that reveal the rationales behind observed behaviors and attitudes, one must take care not to oversimplify. In fact, we nearly always begin our inquiry into how someone views reality by asking people to describe what they consider to be a "bum rap"—a way in which that individual can be misperceived or have his or her behavior misinterpreted. Incidentally, when instructing managers in the skills of comprehending another person's orientation, we often give them a second list of questions designed to help them focus on the themes embedded in the questions they have on their list. These are presented in the list below. This second list helps people think of other areas for discussion that might better reveal what they are attempting to learn.

QUESTIONS TO ORIENT LISTENERS
IN DISCUSSIONS OF PERSONAL ORIENTATIONS

1. What's this person's theme? What's the quest, the struggle, the strength to be demonstrated, the inner fear?

2. How does this person see him- or herself as unique and special and what qualities distinguish his or her participation from that of someone else?
3. What's this person's goal for "existence" in the moment? How does this individual want to "be," to feel, to relate to people and environments? How does this person want to be seen?
4. Where do the opportunities for that moment-by-moment existence and image-making lie? What activities, relationships, or challenges provide the optimal setting for this individual to *be* the way he or she desires, and to be seen the way he or she wants to be seen?
5. What's a "win" or "success" today? What work product, relationship, or tangible result would realize this person's immediate goals?
6. What might be a success tomorrow? What longer-term product would symbolize the realization of this individual's efforts and desire to lead a personally meaningful existence at work and possibly to receive recognition for this?

Notwithstanding the usefulness of the above-mentioned way of proceeding, we know another method of learning about orientations that can be even more effective, particularly in adding trust and confidence to a relationship. This method is less mechanical than going through lists of questions and relies on processes that are more spontaneous, less subject to time constraints, and less dependent on the inquirer being in control. This method requires personal engagement, authenticity, and a genuine liking of people. It requires the use of psychology—not in the sense of "psyching" someone out to get an upper hand, but the use of psychology in being sensitive to where the search for understanding might prove most productive. It also involves the use of psychology in accurately communicating what one hears so that the other person will feel understood and will want to reveal even more.

We call this second method "discrepancy analysis." In our minds it is a variant of the same analytic process on which all social scientists rely. The structure is relatively straightforward: one uses inconsistencies in the patterns of someone's behavior, deviations from what is expected, feelings of discomfort, or any other form of discrepancy that seems to exist as the beginning point for inquiry. Using this method one searches *divergently*, inquiring, "What does the existence of this deviation, feeling, inconsistency, or discrepancy tell me about _____?" with the blank being filled in with "this other person," "myself," "our relationship," "incompatibilities in our self-interests," "the system in which the two of us relate," or anything that seems appropriate to explain the discrepancy that occurred.

Discrepancy analysis assumes that people and their patterns can make sense and that when one individual or one social situation fails to compute in the mind of the person viewing it, the reasons for this failure lie in the fact that an essential characteristic has not yet been accurately perceived and understood—*not* that there is something wrong with the person whose behavior is being questioned. This method assumes that everyone's personal orientation is different, that everyone's view of what must be accomplished is connected to what that person is trying to actualize personally and self-beneficially (the xy factor), and that everyone's view of external situations depends, in great part, on how he or she is attempting to succeed in the high priority items in his or her life overall. The search is to understand what has yet to make sense in the behavior and attitudes one observes.

Viewing discrepancies and analyzing them requires a solid reference point or what there is to learn will have insufficient contrast to be noticed or understood. Contrast is what allows anthropologists to see so much in a foreign culture. The greater the differences between actions taken in one's own culture and actions observed in the culture being studied, the easier it is to see what is assumed as a matter of course in one's own culture but the more difficult it is to interpret the meaning another culture gives to it.

In an organization, an easily accessible reference point is available in the form of the dominant reality, but we don't advise using it as a contrasting framework because it casts one's deviations as violations of standard organization practices and this puts people on the defensive.

We recommend using one's own personal assumptions and one's own ways of doing things as the point of reference. But we recommend doing so only if one can omit the moral imperatives that so often accompany self-statements and justifications of one's actions. That is, when not understanding or not appreciating the actions someone takes, one should avoid questions that communicate disapproval or tones of indignation such as, "Whatever possessed you to _____?" or "For the life of me, I can't understand what you had in mind when you _____?" Instead, one should attempt to make factual statements, something on the order of "I would do it differently; I need to see what you had in mind," or "I don't think we're making the same assumptions; tell me more about what you see as your role and responsibilities," or "I'm beginning to think we're headed in somewhat different directions, and in order to avoid a possible conflict I need to get onboard with you and see what you are planning." One's statements should not reflect any assumption that the other person is all wet, but should take into account that what is missing is insight into where the other person is coming from, the assumptions he or she is making, the context he or she needs to be personally effective, and how what is being observed fits in with the rest of that person's life.

In making these recommendations we recognize that what we are proposing under the label of "discrepancy analysis" is very personal and requires conversations on a different level than many professionals and managers are accustomed to having with work associates. This may make some people uncomfortable, but even so we think this is appropriate for managers who have their minds set on such a personal topic as "motivating" someone. What we are proposing is no more personal than what is discussed during conventional attempts to motivate someone, only we are proposing that these discussions be held in the presence of the person who is to be "motivated." We lack words to express fully our amazement at the things people who are out to motivate you will say about your personal life and conjecture about your innermost thoughts while you are out of the room. As consultants we are often in the room listening to these discussions, usually in the role of attempting to construct more sober rationales for the behaviors managers have decided are inadequacies and the personal defects that they think need to be fixed.

By now our reason for urging that people develop their skills for accurately reading another person's reality should be fairly clear. We want people to appreciate the internal framework that the other person is using before they seek to influence him or her. We are hoping that they will be able to bring the other person's strengths into focus, comprehend the logic that actually drives that person's behavior, and view conflicts in orientation as issues of interpersonal compatibility and organization fit. Many so-called motivation problems are more appropriately dealt with at the level of relationship problems and incompatibility of orientation. Attempts to solve them by sequentially searching for bigger carrots and heavier sticks in order to motivate the other person simply don't work. They only succeed in creating larger rifts in trust and breakdowns in relationships.

To help another person mobilize his or her best efforts and skills in the service of some organizational cause, one must do more than accurately read the other person's reality and comprehend his or her orientation. One must also visualize how that person, with his or her unique orientation, can relate on terms acceptable to him or her. Trusting relationships and a stable organization reality cannot occur when one or more individuals are forced to accept an existing group's strategic reality. For them this already-in-place reality is not strategic; it is *dominant*, and they look for ways to modify it to gain more centrality and focus—context—for what they are about.

Thus, we believe that anyone who thinks about "motivating" someone else should also understand that organizational realities are the result of social agreements, and in order to serve the needs and interests of all the people in a work unit or organization, these agreements must be updated periodically. Without such acceptance, their "motivational" efforts will be experienced as attempts to force conformity, and people who lack context will resist those efforts because their strength and ability to be valued depend on working against this status quo. People who lack context and are perceived as needing someone to "motivate" them are also people who are ever on the alert to modify the dominant reality. And when they are met with tactical approaches aimed at manipulating their needs and preserving the dominant reality, trusting relationships and overlapping pictures of organization events will remain out of reach.

It takes skill to visualize how dominant realities and existing roles can be modified to fit the interests of everyone who is involved. It takes a special sensitivity to visualize how newcomers, or people who lack context, can relate to ongoing group efforts on terms that are acceptable to them without making modifications that upset the other balances that already exist. These skills involve the capacity to monitor several realities at once—to recognize that different people simultaneously experience the same events differently and conceive ways of proceeding that are simultaneously responsive to their different realities. In essence, new strategic realities need to be formed.

We wish we knew how to give a *short* course in visualizing realities that are simultaneously attentive to many people's needs at once. We do know that such an ability demands sensitivity and the discipline to use this sensitivity in ways that benefit others without manipulating them. In the short run people can get away with manipulating; in the long run, manipulations are usually noticed and those perpetrating them are not trusted. If an individual is inclined to take a sensitivity training course to sharpen his or her skills, then we recommend those forms of sensitivity training that emphasize interpersonal skills. Over the years hundreds of thousands of people have gained enormously through their involvement in sensitivity training groups. They have developed both their ability to relate to the realities of others and their ability to consider another person's view of the world when taking action on a project of mutual concern. However, in many organizations sensitivity training experiences are well-kept secrets. People are cautious about revealing the personal competency lessons they needed to learn, particularly when mentioning them calls attention to areas where one still lacks perfection.

Conclusion

In advocating a strategic orientation, we are aware that what we are recommending involves more psychology than is often deemed acceptable in the prevailing management culture and entails interpersonal involvements in areas where many managers doubt their skills. Certainly what we are recommending is imprecise and relies on interpersonal encounters without guarantees that they will yield positive results. Moreover, many executives fear that what we are suggesting, if implemented, will cause the organization to grind progressively to a halt. They reason: "What could be less efficient than a situation where managers and their subordinates sit around analyzing one another all day long?" In response to this reasoning, we would ask "What could be less efficient than managers and subordinates who have little idea of what is behind another's behavior, who find it necessary to spend hours trying to get over their wonderment and resentment of the other person's 'misguided' actions, and to search for organizationally acceptable ways to control, divert, and circumvent the actions and attitudes to which they have just been exposed?''

Of course managers and people of all stripes need to strike a balance between analysis, discussion, and getting the job done. And we are 100 percent in favor of this balance coming out on the side of increasing productivity. Moreover, we would be willing to withdraw all that we have just asserted if only managers would discard their manipulative use of the term "motivation." But if managers want to make corrections in the orientations people use, which after all is their job, and want to do so in a way that attends both to the other person's needs for context and their own desires to create trusting relationships, then they must know how to use psychology and sensitivity, and must be committed to considering the needs and interests of others.

CHAPTER 15

Power

In many respects this entire book is about power. We have described the *personal power* that derives from having an effective alignment. We have described the *organizational power* that derives from having one's needs for context parallel the dominant reality of the organization. We have described power struggles—the conflicts that break out when people disagree about which personally advantageous modification of the dominant organizational reality will best move the organization ahead. And we have hinted at the existence of a strategic power orientation that can breed trust, teamwork, and the spirit of collaboration—even among those whose needs for context and whose relationship with the dominant reality appear to conflict with one's own. Now we are at the point where we can elaborate on what it takes to develop such a collaborative orientation without losing the power to get others to take one's views seriously at moments of one's own choosing.

We've seen the orientation we're about to describe used many times, but by relatively few people. It's a form of power that is totally consistent with what we now know about alignment, people's needs for context, and the basis of reality in an organization. And because it is used by people who have never heard of our concepts, we inquire about it whenever we can. We question users about what leads them to engage others the way they do and

which experiences showed them how. Invariably, their explanations take us back to a formative time in their past. For instance,
listen to what our questioning evoked from a very successful chief
executive whose style is emulated downward through much of his
chain of command. When we asked, he related the following
story.

"I have no doubt that I owe most of the credit for my current
outlook and approach to management to the stormy relationship I had with my first boss, a Frenchman named Robert. I
was twenty-one years old at the time; Robert was nearly fifty.
He had come to London to join my family's import-export
business as a partner and I had just finished college and was
learning the business from the ground up as an order-taker in
the sales department, which Robert was heading.

From the instant I met Robert, I was fascinated with how he
behaved and dealt with people. Immediately I started analyzing the paths that would enable me to achieve his reputation
and popularity. He had a way of making me feel like the center
of the universe. He's one of those guys who, every time he
talks with you, makes insightful observations about your activities and has a rare ability to convey an ever-present interest
in what you are saying. I have never seen him reject an idea or
proposition out of hand. Whenever a difference in opinion
arose, or a disagreement developed between us, he would stop
and analyze the structure of the problem and step by step explore the advantages and disadvantages of both our positions.
When I think of it now, I marvel at his ability to engage other
people's points of view in a respectful manner. Many times I
have heard him say that, given this or that way of seeing
things, the other person was right. He never seemed to have
the need to impose his outlook on others and always seemed
to enjoy and learn from whatever differences might emerge.

A closeness developed between our families and we spent
many weekends together. I was particularly impressed with
the way he played with and interacted with his only child, a
boy who was ten when I first met Robert. But his tolerance for
whatever his child would do puzzled me. His philosophy was
to let people learn by experience. But sometimes I thought
things got out of hand with Pascal. This boy would dismantle
one of Robert's radios and break it and Robert would react

merely by telling him not to do that again. For me, at the time, that was an extreme demonstration of tolerance and patience.

What fascinated me most was Robert's knowledge and culture. He was virtually a living encyclopedia. I would listen for hours to his stories of Van Gogh's madness, the world wars, discoveries in medicine, etc. His way of relating to current and past events affected me greatly. I developed an urge for reading and learning that I never had in college. I realized that I had to be as curious and open-minded as he was if I wanted to impress people as he impressed me. So I started reading books and magazines in an attempt to acquire the same level of knowledge. My attitude was that every subject was interesting. I tried to imitate him and act as harmoniously as possible with other people. I frequently thought, 'What would Robert do in this situation?'

As the months went by my personality and character developed and my admiration of Robert diminished. I started to observe how he behaved with other people. I was disappointed to see that he would use the same flattering remarks with everybody. Now it seemed as if it was his style to push his complimentary attitude to the extreme in a nondiscriminating way. I noticed that the harmonious atmosphere he built around him prevented him from dealing with conflict, and it appeared to me that he was going to extraordinary lengths to avoid fighting. I heard him use the same stories over and over again to make the same point. I sometimes had the feeling that I was hearing a broken record. I started wondering why he would spend so many weekends with my parents and began to suspect that he was unable to be alone with his wife and child and that he needed to have lots of company around him. About this time I developed confidence in my own point of view and began to argue that it was superior to his.

My assignment at the firm changed and that was fine with me. I found myself avoiding Robert. When work necessitated our interaction, I would remain cool and take pains to withhold agreement even if our positions were identical. I don't know to this day whether or not Robert ever understood the rancor hidden in my actions. I felt betrayed and I resented him.

Gradually it dawned on me that my problem was not with Robert but myself. It wasn't Robert who was being indiscriminate, it was me. I was guilty of having imposed on him my needs for perfection and when I saw his failings I began to hate him for misleading me. Then I had to find my own way and that meant denying there was anything valid about Robert's.

It was years later that I discovered how competitive I had become. I had moved to the States and was working for another firm. While I was visiting my family in London, Robert walked in. Suddenly I was confronted with a special man possessing charm, grace, and wonderful insight. And still, in the kindest fashion, he was inserting his view into the conversations in ways that made me feel bigger than life. When I left, I threw my arms around him and kissed him on the cheek. There were tears in my eyes and that was the last time I saw him. He's an old man now and my brother writes that Robert is director emeritus of the family company and that he comes to each meeting ready as ever to participate and guide but never to stir up conflict.

I've come to realize how different I am from Robert. For one thing, I enjoy a good fight. But, like Robert, I also know how to give each person his due and appreciate that the same issue looks totally different to people with different views. And Robert's respect for people and their individual beliefs is a model for me still. Oh, I'm nowhere the person Robert is but apparently enough has rubbed off that I am sometimes aware of others using me as their model. And secretly I wonder how long it will be before someone who tries to emulate me today will experience the inner need to exaggerate my faults just as I needed to do with Robert.''

This executive's story illustrates the three behavioral modes that typify conventional orientations toward power. We label them *power-giving, power-taking* and *power-denying*. Each of these is a mode of operating that, as a young man, this executive passed through en route to a more enlightened mode—one that ultimately paralleled Robert's. We label this enlightened mode *power-sharing*. We call it enlightened because it reflects a collaborative stance that contrasts with the other modes which too often are competitive in their implementation. They don't need to be competitive because in fact, in their collaborative form, they provide the basic ingredients for power-sharing. Allow us to run through them for you.

Power-Giving

Power-giving is the act of viewing the world through another person's framework. It's what people who seek to identify with someone else's power do in a patterned way. It's also what people who seek to empathize with another person do to understand that other person's view and why he or she holds that position.

As a pattern, power-giving entails a yielding of one's own position. It's what happened to the executive in our example when, as a young man, he was enamored with Robert's power to the point that he wanted to fashion himself in its wake. He *gave* Robert the power and in the process he lost his own. With this tack, the best he could hope to become was a replica of Robert. This proved to be personally unsatisfying and just as suddenly as he adopted this style, he gave it up.

Power-giving is harmful when a person judges him- or herself primarily in the framework of someone else's alignment. This proves disorienting and costs one personal power. It leaves an individual evaluating his or her special abilities and organizational commitments in a framework that does not necessarily reflect what that other person has in mind when he or she feels inclined to act one way or another. And it can be harmful to one's organizational power in that it results in an individual putting another person's priorities ahead of what he or she is charged, first and foremost, with accomplishing.

Oftentimes power-giving is a pattern that an individual falls into as a result of others asserting their power. Our students often use the term "taking the test" to indicate that a professor has approached them evaluatively as if they should be making that professor's priorities the foreground of their life. Likewise our clients refer to the "What have you done for me lately?" question that they receive when an evaluator approaches them as if none of their other efforts, contributions, and priorities mattered. Power-giving is promoted when one person makes demands of another with little concern for the realities of that person's life and/or the rest of his or her personal and organizational commitments.

To the extent that a person falls into a power-giving pattern, that person will find him- or herself in a competitive position. However, the competition is not with another person, it is with one's *own* internalization of another person's frame of reference. The competition is between one's desire to incorporate another person's framework and one's own needs to be true to one's self. We speculate that this is why our executive's period of aping Robert was followed by such a strong rejection and denunciation of Robert's power. It was only after this executive had found his own personal bearings that he could once again enjoy what he valued in Robert.

Power-Taking

Power-taking is the most recognizable form of power. It is very simple. It involves nothing more than viewing the world from one's own point of view and frame of reference. It's an orientation that is often rooted in self-affirmation. An individual is confident of his or her own orientation and position in relation to the dominant reality and straightforwardly asserts his or her beliefs and self-conveniently labels each organizational situation.

Everyone in an organization has a stake in developing his or her power-taking skills. They are the crux of what we've been talking about in terms of establishing the context that one needs to be personally and organizationally effective and to have the chance to be a success. In an organization, reality is negotiable and each individual owes it to him- or herself to present others with the road map for appreciating what he or she is up to and why he or she needs to proceed in a given way.

Power-taking is competitive when an individual insists on viewing events strictly from his or her frame of reference without interest in what it would take for someone else, with a different set of personal priorities and work commitments, also to operate with personal and organizational power. This is what our executive did when he was pushing away from Robert. He did more than press his organizational view; he argued that Robert's was inferior. Had Robert been a less mature type, he might have taken up the gauntlet and turned this situation into a nasty organizational fight. In our consulting we've seen hundreds of such incidents—two competent people, defining their operations in fundamentally competitive ways, out to seize each opportunity to discredit the other because the fight had gotten to the point where one needed to get the other before the other got him or her.

Power-Denying

Power-denying is the least recognizable orientation toward power, probably because an individual using this orientation typically keeps his or her objectives hidden. Usually one's objectives include blocking power-taking by another without taking responsibility for having to state an opposing point of view. This is what the executive, as a young man, did when he took a cool attitude with Robert and went through a period of withholding his viewpoint and especially his agreement. He never had to assert another point of view, he simply let Robert's die on the vine for lack of his energy and agreement.

Power-denying is the set of actions that ensures that no one else is allowed to structure reality in a way that robs one of the context that he or she is attempting to establish. It is how one holds off overzealous competitors who are attempting to impose their projects or priorities against one's will without making a personal incident or creating an organizational row. In the most positive sense, power-denying enables an individual to maintain his or her independent point of view without getting embroiled in a fight, resisting what another person asserts. This is a particularly effective practice when one senses that the power-taker will shortly find his or her own way to a more mutually considerate place. In a negative sense, power-denyers are obstructionistic to organizational progress. They stand between someone with an idea and the energy to pursue it and organizational action. We suspect power-denying whenever we get wind of someone blocking an action on what appear to be bureaucratic grounds—where a proposal is being opposed, either on the basis that its form is incorrect or that it violates established policies and procedures, without its spirit and function being engaged.

Power-Sharing

Power-sharing is our term for the orientation toward power that Robert had, that the executive developed, and that creates the type of teamwork that makes an organization soar. It's an orientation that contrasts with conventional approaches toward power in which people attempt to impose their wills on one another. Power-sharing is an orientation that seeks power for the individual but in a far less competitive way. It seeks power in the form of getting other poeple to take one's views seriously, particularly at moments of one's own choosing.

Power-sharing entails using the noncompetitive forms of each of the previously mentioned orientations. It involves elements of power-taking—the ability to state one's views clearly and in a form that shows people enough about one's underlying frame of reference that they understand one's reasons for holding those views. It was only after the executive matured and developed more self-confidence that he learned how to state his position clearly in a way that was also respectful of other people's views. Up until that time he had the concept and the goal but he lacked the internal security to produce the behavior. This was a capacity that Robert already had when the executive met him, and while it served as a model and personal goal, it apparently became the stimulus for competition.

Power-sharing involves elements of power-giving—the ability to view an issue using the internal framework of another individual. This is essential if one ever is to manifest empathy in his or her dealings with others. However, power-giving is very costly if the individual doesn't also have the capacity to simultaneously keep track of his or her own perspective and point of view. Apparently this was the root of the conflict the executive experienced with Robert. He could see Robert's perspective but in the process he lost track of his own. He had to push away from Robert in order to find his own center. Of course power-giving was a wonderfully developed quality of Robert's, one that made this executive feel ''bigger than life.''

Power-sharing involves elements of power-denying—the ability to block domination by the reality of another without creating an ''incident'' or sparking a fight. From the executive's account this seems to be an orientation he always had and one that he perfected with time. We see it undeveloped in the way he denied agreement with Robert when he was pushing away to strengthen his own identity, and we see it better developed when, at the end of his story, he muses about the people who are likely to compete with him. And of course this is a quality that, from the executive's account, Robert seems to have had in abundance, to the extent that Robert would never openly conflict. The executive called this a flaw and criticized Robert's fear of conflict—and probably it was that too. After all, we're talking about orientations, not perfection, and ultimately it's impossible to separate out the strengths of an action from that which is self-protective and helps an imperfect individual cope and get along.

Conventional orientations toward power are competitive at their core. They involve "zero-sum" reasoning in which an increase in one person's power comes at the expense of someone else's. In contrast, the power-sharing orientation requires that a person who "takes" power not take it from someone else, or engage in an act that invalidates the other person, and that the person who "gives" power should do so only if he or she knows how to do it without invalidating him- or herself. A power-sharing orientation allows an individual to say "no" to someone else's proposal or point of view without denying the validity of the frame of reference that produced that person's advocacy.

Power-sharing is an orientation that follows directly from the perspective advanced in this book and which is embodied in the construct *strategic reality*. Recall that a strategic reality is a reality that simultaneously satisfies the context needs of two or more individuals while considering issues that these individuals believe are essential to the well-being of the organization. It requires that someone learn enough about one another's internalized frame of reference to comprehend the context in which that person operates, and that one will develop the respect and motivation to use that context along with his or her own. It's unrealistic to think that someone will give an equal amount of consideration to the context needs of everyone, including him- or herself, who is interested in the outcome of a specific project. However, it is not unrealistic to expect that an individual will develop the sensitivity and commitment to stand responsive to another person's claim that his or her needs for context were not adequately considered, and to be willing to broaden his or her perspective in the face of such enunciation.

Inevitably the question will be asked, "Is it possible for one person to assume a power-sharing orientation unilaterally?" To us the issue is choice, not ideology. That is, while we see power-sharing as a desirable orientation, it's not one that can be implemented easily in the competitive environments in which organizational members so often find themselves. During the period when Robert was a steadfast power-sharer and the young executive was in the mode of power-taking, Robert's power-sharing stance cost him consideration for his viewpoint. Had the stakes been higher and had Robert felt consideration for his viewpoint essential to his job security, one wonders what he should have done. Most of us know what we would do if we found ourselves in a high stakes competition with the ability to overpower our opponent. On the other hand, had Robert not been a steadfast power-sharer during the periods of competition and attack, this executive might never have learned about Robert's integrity and the personal power of his approach.

For us power-sharing is a goal. It's a goal that probably can only be realized after people experience each of the other three power orientations and make the transition from their competitive forms to their collaborative ones. While competing, one's personal and organizational power comes at the expense of others and hence at the expense of the general well-being of the organization. Each person's stance sets up the conditions that evoke competitive forms of power-taking, power-giving, and power-denying from each person encountered.

Power-sharing provides a model for thinking strategically. It provides a way of thinking about what people are up to when one sees them pushing their interests at the expense of others, and about the developmental sequence that people must pass through on their way to improved modes of functioning. It provides a model for how people can conduct themselves when either psychologically or situationally they find themselves positioned to assume a collaborative orientation. It would be awful to think that people might wind up at high levels of an organization, or in states of high personal security, and not have a model for operating on which to spend their prosperity. In organizations people do "make it" and power-sharing provides a way of thinking and orienting that allows those who do so to leverage their well-being.

Conclusion

CHAPTER 16

The Cost of Rational Management

This book has already covered many of the costs, limitations, and missed opportunities associated with today's overly rational management. However, we have yet to address the main cost head on:

> THE RATIONAL MODEL MAKES IT POSSIBLE FOR INDI- VIDUALS TO SUCCEED WHILE THE ORGANIZATIONS FOR WHICH THEY WORK LOSE OUT; THE RATIONAL MODEL ALLOWS PEOPLE TO JUSTIFY WHAT THEY ARE DOING WHILE KEY COMPONENTS OF THEIR OPERA- TION RUN DEFICIENTLY.

Almost all managers with troubled organizations, almost all supervisors with work unit problems, and almost all work associates embroiled in conflict can document their production and justify their value. They can all produce the "hard" data that show how their operation's problems would go away if only others would grasp their priorities and rally to support them. And while such accounts inevitably suggest self-serving justifications, the construct of alignment alerts us to the fact that, in most instances, such portrayals are basically correct. If only *others* were better attuned to the unique way one is attempting to produce results and be effective, and would reorient themselves to support it, then that person's organizational unit would, in fact, function with enhanced effectiveness. But, as we have illustrated over and over again, each individual has his or her own personal interests to actualize and is not about to abandon them in the service of merely adding to someone else's effectiveness.

Thus, in our minds, the main problem with the rational model is that it allows people to form personally effective alignments and to defend them even when their orientations fail to fit well with the needs of the people with whom they interact. It permits people to operate with minimal sensitivity to the ways work associates and teammates are attempting to contribute. It permits people to avoid responsibility for creating the conditions that make others effective. In short, it allows people who are producing "results" to put their needs ahead of the overall well-being of the system, and renders management helpless to insist otherwise.

In contrast, the *radical* model requires that management develop sensitivity to the subjective forces which operate at many organizational levels and attempt to orchestrate each individual's alignment and orientation toward the organization's overall success. It assumes that organization effectiveness is produced when people with different alignments who work together realize what each of the others is attempting to contribute, and consciously consider what personal accommodations and adjustments they can make in the spirit of creating an integrated effort. In the radical model, it is management's job to get the system to operate effectively while at the same time creating the conditions that allow individuals with different alignment needs to succeed. And it is management's job to ensure that individual contributions that make the system more effective are valued, scored, and adequately rewarded.

Skills to decode and respect the subjective element are what managers operating with a rationalistic mind-set most critically lack. Without these skills, solving problems is like playing cards without a full deck. Situations involving subjectivity arise, but management lacks the orientation to acknowledge their presence and is stuck either misframing problems or forcing solutions which, at best, are only partially correct. Some of the critical skills lacked by managers operating with the rationalistic mind-set are:

1. *Skills to decode and respect the subjective interests of each individual.* The rationalistic mind-set leads managers to specify what they have the "right" to require from a specific performer, regard-

less of that individual's capacity to produce it or to deliver it in the specified form. It creates situations where people are criticized for what they are not doing well and not given credit for what they, in fact, could contribute if only things were structured somewhat differently.

In contrast, managers using the *radical* perspective search out the unique attributes an individual is striving to express and emphasize in the way he or she performs, comprehend how such expression can make that individual personally powerful, and engineer situations so that the organization can capitalize on what that individual does best.

2. *Skills to decode and respect the way the system actually functions.* Managers who use the rationalistic mind-set get caught up thinking with a logic that mirrors the "formal" needs of the system. As a result, they communicate in a rhetoric that can disorient those who listen to them. The rationalistic mind-set mistakes "shoulds" for actual operating assumptions and leads managers to hold others accountable on performance dimensions that in actuality are immaterial to what the organization needs accomplished in order to operate effectively.

In contrast, the *radically* oriented manager comprehends the subjective interests of the organization and can separate the needs of actual practice from publicly stated "shoulds." What's more, the radically oriented manager is intent on demystifying the system and on realistically discriminating between the logic that describes what people idealize and expect, and the practices that actually characterize what people do.

3. *Skills to decode and respect the behavior of an individual who lacks a meaningful relationship with the system.* Managers spend a significant portion of their time coping with the dynamics created by individuals with alignment problems who are attempting to satisfy their political and context needs. When an apparent mismatch between the needs of an individual and the needs of the system occurs, the rationally oriented manager is inclined to take the system's needs as a given and work to get the individual to conform.

In contrast, the *radically* oriented manager understands that both the needs of the individual and the needs of the system are at least somewhat mutable and attempts to discover what adaptations can produce a mutually productive fit. He or she comprehends the importance of people finding a solid connection between the pursuit of their needs and the pursuit of the system's interests, and the inevitability of political behavior when one does not exist.

The costs of operating with the rational model are dramatically illustrated in an account of a rationally thinking manager who did his absolute best to manage his department "correctly." When we met Doug, he was head of the department of international engineering for a major U.S. company, a position he had held for two years.

Doug had succeeded an autocratic manager whose style, he felt, had cost the organization considerably. He inherited six section heads whose lack of spontaneity and "What should I do next, boss?" attitude deprived his department of energy, verve, and commitment. His subordinates never argued about what needed to be done; instead, they worried about what the boss, now Doug, thought and wanted.

Doug decided to take the initiative. In an effort to generate more spark and creativity he instituted what he called a "management-by-results" program. At six-month intervals, Doug would sit down with each section head and inquire into that person's projects and how he planned to go about accomplishing them.

Next Doug would add his ideas, attempt to stimulate some give-and-take discussion, and strike an agreement regarding the tangible outcomes that might reasonably be achieved in each important area of performance. Doug's goals were to give his section heads more latitude to act between checkpoints with him, to revise his own daily role to one of coach and consultant, and to create a system whereby section heads, and the project engineers working for them, asserted more initiative and took more responsibility for getting jobs accomplished.

It took three cycles for Doug to get his "management-by-results" program to where he thought it should be. Understandably the section heads were cautious. During the first cycle, Doug prodded them to take some risks and to commit to goals that were not fail-safe, against which real achievement could be measured. During the second cycle, the achievements of the first round were noted, and Doug found himself on the other side of the fence counseling his section heads against overcommitment and setting themselves up for needless failures. By the time the third cycle was in place, the section heads were taking Doug into their confidence, discussing their weaknesses with him, asking his help on goals *they* initiated, and requiring less attention in the way of daily instructions. Two more cycles and the system was working well enough for Doug to use these six-month reviews to determine merit pay increases.

Suddenly, in the midst of what appeared to be a smooth-sailing process a problem emerged that shook Doug's confidence in the appropriateness of his approach. The problem, over which Doug was still puzzling when he sought our counsel some ten months later, centered on the selection of a temporary replacement for himself.

Doug had been assigned to supervise the building of a prototype plant in Mexico, which, his boss explained, would require three to five months full-time on site, with periodic follow-up visits. Doug's instinct was to continue his department-head responsibilities from Mexico, but his boss prevailed upon him not to dilute his Mexico involvement with concern for issues that were better handled at headquarters. He was told to "let go" and designate a temporary replacement.

According to Doug, the management-by-results records should have provided his replacement's name. However, his top-scorer was a man whose opinionated statements made Doug's boss uneasy and whose style was still too abrupt for Doug to feel comfortable with; Doug couldn't fathom coming back and living with the aftermath. As he looked down the list, Doug realized that the only section head to whom he could comfortably entrust his department stood fourth in terms of the *objective* management-by-results measures. Selecting him, however, would undermine both Doug's and his system's credibility.

Doug claimed he solved his problem "creatively." He did so by recruiting a section head from outside his group who worked for his counterpart in domestic engineering. In order to reduce the awkwardness of not selecting an insider, Doug let it be known that the individual selected was being "cross-trained" on the "international side of the house" for future managerial assignments.

Doug told us that he left for Mexico with queasy feelings. As he later analyzed it, his management-by-results program had produced a situation in which:

1. The top-scoring person was not someone to whom he could comfortably entrust his department, particularly

when he would have to come back and live with the results.

2. He had to bypass the section head whom he felt was most qualified to succeed him because that person had not scored high enough on Doug's "objective" management-by-results measures.

3. He had been forced to choose a replacement with whom he had no firsthand knowledge over people whose strengths and weaknesses were intimately known by him.

4. He saw no alternative but to fabricate an imaginative cover story in order to justify the actions he needed to take in order to best serve the company's interests.

Of course, at the time, Doug did the best he could to solve the situation he faced, given the rational variables he had at his disposal.

As it it turned out, Doug's worst fears were realized anyway. Five months later when he returned from Mexico, he found that his section heads had reverted to their former passive ways, and this time he found that virtually nothing he did could regenerate their enthusiasm. This was the situation facing Doug when he buttonholed us after attending an executive seminar of ours.

That Doug had to recruit an "unknown" outsider and fabricate a story to support his doing so were problems worthy of our attention but were not issues which became our principal concern. Of greater concern was the fact that Doug's actions compelled section heads to withdraw their efforts to form organizationally responsive alignments. Only after Doug appointed an outsider did the section heads learn his actual "grading" system. In response, the section heads saw the need to be more self-protective. They reverted to producing results the system would be sure to recognize irrespective of the specific manager in charge.

That such a retreat occurred is no surprise to us; it is a corollary consequence of even the best rationalistic approach. Sooner or later, the subjective issues that are not being dealt with by the rational model surface and this produces the circumstances that cause people to put their needs for success ahead of the system's overall effectiveness. This was the posture Doug found the section heads assuming when he first took over the leadership of international engineering. He saw the section heads "succeeding" by passively giving their autocratic boss everything he wanted. However, he saw their success coming at the cost of the organization's effectiveness: the section heads were not thinking things through and making their own proposals for what was needed. This was also the situation Doug encountered when he returned from Mexico. Again the section heads were "succeeding" by producing results everyone had to respect. This time, they were using Doug's management-by-results logic to extract before-the-fact commitments that if they did this, this, and that, they would then be rewarded. In different ways each had assumed a self-protective and conformist orientation, asking precise questions and generally operating on an "I'm not going to make a mistake" basis. Risk taking and creativity had evaporated from their behavior.

Doug had tried to produce organizational effectiveness by encouraging each section head to say what he thought the organization needed and by putting enough "English" on what the section head said to get a commitment to how Doug thought that section could function best. Unfortunately, Doug never made his own desires and standards clear enough for his section heads to receive an accurate picture of what the system actually required. In fairness, Doug may have explained things the best way he could and only discovered his own subjective preferences after the fact when he was faced with making a decision that held personal consequences for him. In either case, Doug's commitment to the rational model deprived him of the insight to stay out of trouble. Either Doug did not adequately comprehend the role his own subjective interests played in determining what he ultimately called the "objective" standards of the system, or he did not want to put himself on the line by stating them and risk being seen as biased.

To us, Doug's story is but one more example of how the rational model underestimates the inevitability of subjective forces and the inadequacy of managerial actions that do not address these forces explicitly. The rational model conveys the impression that there is a predefined set of attributes and orientations people should possess, that when they have them their organizations will be successful, and when they lack them, their organizations will have serious problems. In contrast, the *radical model* specifies that what makes an organization successful is great fits between imperfect human beings—who can do some things very well—and functions that can be performed in many ways—and ought to be performed in the unique way the individual can perform them best.

The radical model specifies that the key to an organization's success lies in management's capacity to decode the subjective element and make it work for the betterment of the organization. Decoding includes: (1) the capacity to ascertain the uniquely personal dimensions on which an individual performs best, and to respectfully note weaknesses that could cause work effectiveness problems; (2) the capacity to comprehend both the subjective interests of the managers who represent the organization and the latitudes in operational style that might exist; and (3) the capacity to propose adjustments that allow imperfect people to form organizationally desirable alignments without compromising the power and potential of the individual or essential subjective facets of the system.

At its core, the radical model assumes that the subjective interests of each individual are unknowns until one makes the effort to learn specifically what they are. It assumes that organizations and systems have subjective dimensions and latitudes in operation that cannot be comprehended or predicted until they are questioned with respect to a particular individual who has specific talents, limitations, and needs for context.

Conversely, the rational model specifies that the key to an organization's success lies in management's capacity to specify the skills, attitudes, and motivations that people should possess and to create the systems that practically capitalize on this knowledge. In the rational model, it is management's job to carefully plan, implement, and control against deviations. Management attempts to maintain control by establishing a set of conditions that make it harder for people who deviate from their plan to stay in the organization without paying a price.

Like those who use the radical model, managers using the rationalistic approach also inquire into the frameworks of others and frequently, like Doug, put enormous energy and commitment into doing so. However, what Doug, or any rationally oriented manager, can see is limited by the model that person uses. No matter how long a manager inquires, or how deeply he or she delves, a model that does not disclose the active and dynamic role subjectivity plays in a subordinate's basic orientation to all organization events—what we're calling "alignment"—severely limits the adequacy of that manager's organizational response. In our story,

Doug learned about his section heads' goals. But he did not comprehend why individual section heads felt the need to proceed as they did, nor did he reveal enough about his and his boss's orientations to develop an adequate dialogue about the discrepancies between the section heads' orientations and his own.

How would the radical management model have helped? *First,* it would have led Doug to be more up front. Instead of playing a cat and mouse game over six-month intervals, Doug would have, early on, held focused discussions to learn more about each section head's personal and professional goals and needs. He would have held explicit discussions about their areas of responsibility and how their needs, interests, values, and skills might best be expressed. He would have gotten inputs from his boss and relevant others, and then created his beginning plan. By describing his plan he would have presented section heads with the blueprint of his desires. Then there would have been discussions to negotiate details—opportunities for section heads to modify their needs, and opportunities for Doug to explore the flexibility in his system. In this radical model, Doug's plan and organization would be created according to the realities of the individuals involved. And in this model individual section heads could score Doug's management effectiveness against their knowledge that he was aware of the professional directions they individually would like to take.

Second, with his plan in mind, Doug would have sought to transfer out section heads who didn't appear to have a good up-front fit with what he envisioned being accomplished. For a section head, there is no failure implied in being transferred because a new boss's needs and orientation are a poor fit with his or her own. In stating this we by no means want to imply that we champion a doppelganger theory of management whereby each person is encouraged to become a miniature of the boss. To the contrary, the radical management approach recognizes the uniqueness of each individual, emphasizes complementarity of effort, and is realistic enough to note that, for factors too numerous to list, certain people don't match up well. What's more, a boss who notices a poor fit before the fact is ideally situated to broker a transfer by presenting the mismatched person as just that. Conversely, a boss with six months or more of disappointed expectations is in a bind about how to unload the "damaged goods."

Third, the radical management approach eventually leads to team meetings. These meetings emphasize problem identification and problem solving, not just information exchange. Such meetings would require that section heads take a department-wide perspective and participate with more than their individual section management needs in mind. That is, team meetings are only effective when subordinates consider issues from the standpoint of the good of the entire group. Of course any team participation is advisory to the boss and the boss who mistakes group opinion for governance is, in our minds, on his or her way to receiving a severance check.

Participation in team problem-solving meetings can go far to create feelings of trust, self-confidence, and fairness even when individuals are disappointed in not getting a particular job, role, or promotion. Team participation of the type prescribed in the radical management approach provides people with the experience of examining issues with consideration for the other person's alignment and point of view. People understand the reasoning behind a decision even when their self-interests lead them to disagree with the outcome. Such a forum would have helped Doug considerably. Section heads would have known his subjective preferences right along, and they would have appreciated the qualifications of Carl—the section-head Doug would have liked to choose, but couldn't because of the "objective" performance indices that had been used.

A Final Perspective

As we said at the beginning, this is a "how to comprehend" book, not a "how to" book. Of course, enhanced comprehension of organization events is the staging ground for more effective "how to" scenarios. Our objective has been to present concepts and dimensions that change the way readers look at work situations, and hence, to change the nature and priorities of the problems they tackle. Changing the problem is radical. Tackling the same old problems over and over again with the same approach limits the progress managers can make, and perpetuates the status quo.

It would be a mistake for us to leave readers with the impression that we don't value "how tos." But "how tos" come *after* one has decided what the problem is and, as we've maintained all along, organizational problems are determined more by the concepts and perspectives people use in approaching them than they are by any "objective" portrayal of events. As much as any factor, we see problems as statements of unfulfilled expectations. They are primarily a function of unmet alignment needs and unrealized expectations of the negotiated dominant reality. In other words, problems depend on the subjective needs and negotiated interests that precede their formulations.

As a "how to comprehend" book, *Radical Management* attempts to focus managers on new and more basic organizational effectiveness opportunities. We believe that, in many ways, managing with the radical perspective is easier. Certain problems don't come up, some that do can be dealt with on more honest terms so that cover-ups for an individual's imperfections are not necessary, and many problems, particularly relating to politics, trust, and the individual's need for context, can be comprehended more completely. Of course, taking up the radical management perspective is not without its difficulties. There are more variables to consider, there are new problems such as finding ways to access subjective information efficiently, and fewer prescriptions and "how tos" are available to guide one's efforts.

The radical perspective empowers managers in ways that the rationalistic does not. With the *radical* perspective, a manager understands that the way he or she represents the organization's reality is strongly influenced by his or her own subjective interests. When clashes of interest arise, the radical perspective provides a manager with a good degree of latitude and flexibility of response.

On the other hand, a manager with a rationalistic perspective fails to appreciate the ways his or her own needs color the reality he or she communicates; this creates problems in trust. What that manager communicates doesn't fit with other people's experience, and they are put off by that manager's response.

With the *radical* perspective, a manager has a relatively easy time giving others information about the nature of his or her commitments and interests, information that others can use as a guide to understanding the reality they "objectively" have to face.

On the other hand, a manager with a rational perspective periodically gets caught up in a conceptual rhetoric that, despite the number of words used, makes it impossible for him or her to get the point across. Others can't decipher where that manager is coming from and can't figure out what he or she is trying to accomplish with the rational points they hear advanced.

With the *radical* perspective, a manager respects that each subordinate has something unique and special to express which cannot long be subordinated to any organizational rationale. The radical manager understands the needs for compromise, sacrifice, and trade-offs, and is positioned to recognize the spectrum of what an individual contributes.

On the other hand, a manager with a rational perspective is apt to put primary energy into prescribing the ways a subordinate should operate in order to be effective. The rational-thinking manager drives hard bargains in the spirit of benefiting the organization and then spends enormous energy trying to hold people to them.

With the *radical* perspective, a manager understands that subjective expression is essential and that organizational effectiveness depends on people modifying the structure of situations so that their own subjective needs can be met.

On the other hand, a manager with a rational perspective is inclined to hold out for the prescribed structure and discipline. That manager does so because he or she is primarily focused on the problems created by changing them, and does not see the opportunities.

Earlier we likened the rationalistic model to playing a game of cards without a full deck, an analogy to which we can now add. The less competent players continue playing the game as specified and are slow to discover that elements essential to their successful execution are missing. The more competent players figure out what they are missing because they cannot accomplish what they set out to do. These managers deal with their dilemmas by changing the goals of their game. They then communicate the changes and carry on. But their goals are now based on what they can achieve, not on what they set out to accomplish. To us this is both the genius and the weakness of the American management system. Managers accept the cards they are dealt and attempt to cope and win. But in such a steadfast commitment to coping, managers pervert the "game" they set out to play. Radical management seeks to go back to the original game and fill in the "deck" with that which was inadvertently left out.

What was left out was the subjectivity that is inherent in every organizational act, an element we include with the construct *alignment*. It is ironic that this term is used in a radical context, for alignment is a construct that gives order to the potpourri of subjective forces that actually determine the course of each organizational event. It accomplishes the rationalist's need for order, stability, and predictability. The extent to which *alignment* is thought of as radical bespeaks a generation of overly rational managers who lack models for dealing realistically with subjectivity. Rational-thinking managers have always acknowledged some subjectivity, the subjectivity that links one's work involvement to extrinsic factors such as money, power, and status. But rational-thinking managers lack a way of linking intrinsic quests for meaning to how people actually perceive each event at work and how people actually perform each activity. They lack ways of conversing directly and respectfully about conflicts in self-interests, about the ways people are attempting to restructure work situations to make them more personally satisfying, and about how an individual's personal sensitivities obstruct certain relationships. Because the radical perspective creates the capacity to comprehend such basic issues, these insights and conversations become possible.

Glossary

Alignment: The individualistic way in which a person orients to work events. It reflects an individual's attempt to maximize expression of the subjective, and the personally important, while producing work he or she believes the organization should receive from someone in his or her job and position.

Context: A viewer's beliefs about the needs, circumstances, and consequences that surround an individual's actions in a particular setting at a particular point in time. In organizations, people struggle to get others to view their actions in the "proper context"—the one they personally use in attributing meaning and value to the actions they take, usually framed to emphasize a consistency between what they are doing and what others believe is organizationally acceptable.

Discrepancy analysis: A method of developing information about another person's actual motivations that is based on what the viewer sees as flaws, inconsistencies, and/or disorientation in that person's behavior.

Dominant reality: The mainstream organization reality that evolves over time. The "objective" standards referred to when stating the "organizationally acceptable" way of doing things and when arbitrating differing points of view. This reality overlaps various facets of what specific individuals believe but seldom, if ever, encompasses the beliefs of a single individual.

Founder's reality: An idealized reality formed by a group of founders pooling their self-interested visions of what they'd like the organization to be, and striking agreements that lead to a composite picture (of reality) to which each is personally and openly committed.

Fragmenting: Telling that version of the "truth" (as the individual knows it) that is best calculated to produce the self-interested outcomes an individual desires.

Framing: Portraying events to feature one personally convenient interpretation or course of action rather than another.

Motivating (someone): Helping an individual to mobilize his or her unique strengths in the service of an organizational cause that has purpose and meaning to that individual. This definition contrasts with traditional management practices which often entail using one's superior position to dominate an individual and to force a subordination of that person's self-interests to the needs of the organization as perceived by the "motivator."

On-line (action): The action an individual appears to take spontaneously without interrupting the immediate flow of dialogue or events. This contrasts with "off-line" whereby people retreat from ongoing events to calculate how they will stage their proposals and respond to challenges their actions elicit.

Organization politics: The actions, machinations, and dynamics that take place as people strive to create acceptance either for themselves or for a point of view to which they are committed. The objective is to implant a view of reality that elicits a favorable response for one's views and actions. In organizations people are often unaware of their political behavior. However, they are unusually aware of how someone else's framing of reality is making it more difficult for them to get value and acceptance for their behavior and "organizationally constructive" point of view. In response they experience the need to assert another view (of reality) and the resulting dynamics constitute organization politics.

Organizational power: The power that derives from having overlap between the standards that guide one's behavior when performing with excellence and the standards used by the organization to reward performance.

Organization reality: Beliefs about the meaning of events and the responses that should follow which people who work together either jointly hold or individually acknowledge as the prevailing reality of the organization.

Personal power: The power that results from having an effective alignment that the individual perceives as producing valuable product for the organization.

Playing it both ways: Words and actions that give the false impression that one is sympathetic to the views and course advocated by the speaker which allows one to avoid exposing conflicting attitudes, beliefs, and actions.

Power: The ability to get others to respectfully consider one's views, objectives, and different perspectives at moments of one's choosing. This contrasts with the traditional definition which limits "power" to the ability to impose one's will on others. Our version takes issue with the organizational constructiveness of coercing those whose collaborative participation and good will are essential to the success of one's projects.

Power-denying: A response that has the effect of blocking or deflecting the impact of viewpoints that someone else asserts without making the disagreement explicit.

Power-giving: An act of viewing an organizational situation or event from a vantage point or perspective that reflects someone else's framework, perhaps to the exclusion of one's own.

Power politics: The use of behind-the-scenes tactics to make others give a friendly reading to—or at least appear to support—an individual and that individual's projects and causes. Most often this involves the embedding of one's personal and self-interested needs and perceptions in an advocacy that emphasizes what's good for the organization.

Power-sharing: A collaborative power orientation that embodies noncompetitive forms of power-taking, power-giving, and power-denying. With a power-sharing orientation, an individual recognizes that everyone needs context and builds relationships on the understanding that the most efficient way to get others to take his or her point-of-view seriously (take the power) is by demonstrating real interest and respect in their point of view as well (give the power).

Power struggle: The conflict that breaks out when people disagree about which personally advantageous modification of the dominant reality will best move the organization ahead.

Power-taking: Asserting a view of an organizational situation or event that is primarily grounded in one's own internal framework, usually without active concern for the self-interests and context needs of others who are also involved.

Shared fate: The management approach that traditionally has been used in work settings to produce trust. Using this method, management structures goals, incentives, and punishments so that groups of people experience themselves as having a common set of organizational objectives and see themselves gaining personally through cooperation with one another.

Strategic orientation: An orientation to organization events in which the individual works to structure reality in ways that allow him or her to operate with strength in the long term. People who operate strategically are, at the same moment, active in seeking positive, congruent, mutually trusting relationships and sensitive to the need to avoid the snares produced by people whose inclinations for structuring reality are competitive with theirs.

Strategic reality: A reality that simultaneously satisfies the context needs of two or more organizational members and the issues that these individuals believe are essential to the productivity of the organization. This reality is the result of people with divergent needs and expectations communicating with one another and acknowledging the existence of one another's needs and organizational priorities when they frame the institution's reality.

Symbolic events: Organizational events whose outcomes are interpreted as having broader and more general implications for the system and for the individuals involved. Symbolic events are moments when specific actions and attitudes are read more for their value as a sign of things to come than for their immediate impact on the organizational instance at hand.

Tactical orientation: An orientation towards organization events in which an individual seeks to make the most of the circumstances that present themselves in a way that maximizes one's outcomes from the current exchange.

Tactical reality: A structuring of reality or achievement of context that satisfies one individual's self-interested needs, without regard for the needs of others. Tactical realities tend to be unstable—those whose needs are not met will be alert to opportunities to reverse their disadvantage by making modifications in the dominant reality that, in turn, come at the first individual's expense.

Trust: A confidence people extend to others whom they see as having the ability to view them in the proper context, and the willingness to search out and respect that context at moments when differences in self-interests and job orientation place them in competition.

Win-lose approach: An orientation in which people advance either their own or the organization's interests at the expense of the other.

Win-win approach: An orientation that leads people to seek definitions of the organization reality that link their desires for the proper context to the needs and general well-being of the organization.

Win-win-win approach: An orientation that leads people to seek definitions of the organization reality that simultaneously link their desires for the proper context, and the desires of one or more colleagues possessing somewhat different needs for context, to the needs and general well-being of the organization.

Index